6 FIGURE TRUCKING:

You're only one step away from $150k

MAURICE SANDERS

Table of Contents

Section I 3

Introduction 3

Part 1 — The Industry 5

Part 2 — Basic steps to obtaining your CDL.............................24

Part 3 — Surviving your first year 27

SECTION II 38

SECTION III 72

Chapter 1: Pros & Cons Of Owning A Trucking Company 72

Chapter 2: Steps For Starting Your Authority 78

Chapter3: Finding Freight 87

Chapter 4: Negotiating Rates 97

Chapter 5: Paperwork And Documentation 103

Chapter 6: Ongoing Fmcsa And Dot Compliance...................106

Chapter 7: Consortiums And Drug Testing 114

Chapter 8: Your first year and seasoning your authority.......123

Section I

Introduction

I was sitting in the basement of my home playing Madden '11, and my younger brother mentioned that he was going to leave his current job to go to truck driving school. A place that I was three months behind on mortgage payments. I had exhausted loans from family members to make those mortgage payments. To put gas in the car for the week, my wife would go into the negative on her bank account. We used her bank account because I couldn't get a bank account, and I was living payday loan to payday loan, which is worse than check to check. I was struggling as a real estate agent. I had only earned $12,000 in commissions that year, which sounds terrible until I add the fact that I had $15,000 in business expenses. I was on the brink of bankruptcy. I wasn't happy or in love with my wife, and I was on the edge of divorce. I was in a dark place after the passing of my mom. I had blown through an inheritance that included two homes that were free and clear, $35,000 in bank savings, and $150,000 in retirement savings. I was delusional about what I could accomplish with my 2011 mindset. I was horrible at making money, and worse yet, I was awful at saving money. So on the rare occasion where I did get my hands on some cash. I'd blow it. I had big dreams and big aspirations, but I didn't have a realistic plan to accomplish those goals. I was a bad fit for my chosen profession.

When I look at the world, I see dollar signs and opportunity. I knew that trucking that would allow me to provide for my family—a primary goal of mine. But more importantly, trucking could give me a blueprint to build a million-dollar business.

Fast forward to Christmas Eve, and my wife told me she was having an affair with someone that was "not enough of a stranger" " and I moved in with my Aunt. So now I have no wife, no home. My only possession of any value was my car, a '91 Lexus LS 400. I loved that car, but like everything else in my life at the time. Everything was either broken or on its way to being broken. The car's engine overheated, and now I didn't even have a car. I forgot to mention that my license was about to be suspended in the next few weeks.

Fast forward to 15 months after several conversations about trucking with everyone that I knew; I enrolled in truck driving school. I started down a path that would change my life. I went from not having enough to pay my bills to make so much money that I had to find smarter ways to spend my money. I remember two distinct phrases from that time. I spoke with an older gentleman at a bar who had his CDL, and he called it the "Blue Collar Degree" and my girlfriend at the time calling it my stupid truck obsession. Looking back on it, I was obsessed, and whenever you truly want to make life-altering changes, you have to be obsessed!

Part 1 — The Industry

You may be asking yourself why should you pursue a career in commercial truck driving?

Hopefully, by the end of this section, you will have enough valuable information to answer it yourself. Let me start by giving you some fascinating statistics about the trucking industry.

Did you know that of all the modes of shipment in the commercial transportation industry, the trucking sector dominates the field with 83.7% of the revenue? The rail industry comes in at a distance second with only 5.6% of the total revenue. The air sector is third with 3.2%, and the oceanic freight sector is barely in the running with only 1.4% of all revenue being transported by ships. As you can see, the trucking industry isn't going away anytime soon. In fact, the trucking industry alone collects 650 billion dollars in annual revenue each year. That's 5% of the nation's GDP! The trucking industry also pays out 35 billion dollars in federal, state, and highway use taxes per year and will grow by 21% over the next ten years. Not many career fields can promise you such great job security without a four year college degree like the trucking industry can.

Speaking of job security, in May of 2013 there was an estimated 1.5 million heavy truck and tractor trailer drivers earning an average median salary of $38,700 a year, which calculates to roughly $18.61 an hour. In fact, the Bureau of Labor Statistics estimates that truck drivers who were at the lower end of the pay scale still made $25,330 a year and truck drivers who were at the high end of the pay scale made $59,620 per year. How many other jobs can boast such a wide range of salaries without a four-year or two-year college degree? Not many. So, where are more truck drivers employed than anywhere else? Texas, California, Pennsylvania, Florida, and Illinois. The state of Texas hired 157, 260 truckers in 2013 while Illinois employed an estimated 66,050 truck drivers. But, don't think you will have to relocate to one of these five states in order to find a decent truck driving job. The entire east coast is full of states that have an average 40,210 to 157,260 working truck drivers. If you're looking for the states with the highest concentration of truck driving jobs in the U.S. look no further. North Dakota boasts 15,310 trucking jobs with an average median salary of $47,580 while Arkansas, Nebraska, Iowa, and Wyoming follow closely. Truck drivers in Alaska have the highest median salary at $53,440, while truckers in North Dakota, Massachusetts, District of Columbia, and Wyoming make an average $47,000 a year. If you were to look at a map of the United States showing the areas where the most truck drivers are employed, you would see that truck drivers are heavily employed from

6

Texas all the way over to Pennsylvania and Florida, and all the way up to Michigan. Califonia and the Pacific Northwest also employ many truck drivers. Which areas have the least amount of working truck drivers? The midwestern states. That is why truck drivers in these states make more per year. Here's one more thing to consider. U.S. intracontinental truck driving jobs cannot be outsourced.

Here are some more fascinating facts about truckers. The total distance traveled by truck drivers per year is 93.5 million highway miles? To put that in perspective, that's 256,197,260 miles per day, 2,965 milers per second, and 3.7 million times around the earth or 195,713 round trips to the moon! That's a lot of truckin'! Of course, with all those miles it would be nice to get good gas mileage. Unfortunately, that's not going to happen. On average, long haul trukcs can carry 300 gallons of fuel, but can only travel eight miles per gallon. That's about 6.8 gallons of fuel an hour at 55 miles per hour. That means it would take a class 8 tractor trailer 44 hours and 347 gallons of fuel to travel from Los Angeles to New York City. Of course, with a 300 gallon fuel tank, you would only have to stop for gas one time. With all those miles to travel, one of the perks of long haul truck driving is being able to see the beauty and splendor of the United States countryside and getting paid to do so!

The value of shipped goods that the commercial trucking industry transports per year is $139,463,000,000. That's $382,090,411 per day and $4,422 per second! That is how valuable the trucking industry and the truck drivers themselves are to the citizens of the United States. Think about this, if you will. Almost every facet of our economy is dependent upon the trucking industry, from food to fuel, medicine to machinery, cars to clothing, and construction to manufacturing, they are all delivered and dependent upon the commercial trucking industry. To put it another way, if it wasn't for truck drivers, you wouldn't have a bed to sleep on, soap and shampoo to clean yourself with, clothes to get dressed in, food to eat for breakfast, a toothbrush and toothpaste to brush your teeth with, a car to drive to work in, gas to fuel that car, a computer to work on, food to eat for lunch, a car to drive back home in, a refrigerator, stove and microwave to store and cook dinner with, plates and utensils and a table to eat on, chairs to sit on, and a television to watch the game on while you sit in your sofa and drink your ice cold beer that was transported by truck drivers. Of course, I left a lot of stuff out but, you get the picture. Oh, I almost forgot, you wouldn't have a house to live in either, unless it was made out of something other than bricks, concrete, wood, metal, or stone. Remember, if you bought it, a truck brought it.

Not only is the commercial truck driving job market ripe with possibilities, the steps you have to take to enter the job market are easier than you might think. To be certified to operate a commercial motor vehicle, all you need is a commercial drivers license, adequate physical health, and the ability to operate a commercial motor vehicle. That's it. Of course, getting your CDL is a whole different story. It takes specialized knowledge and training to pass the re⊠uired tests, and that training is usually obtained at a private or company-sponsored truck driving school. Most truck driving schools will give you the CDL training you need to pass the re⊠uired CDL tests and obtain your commercial drivers license in as little as a 3 weeks.

Hiring Student Drivers Cuts Costs

Another point to consider is that hiring student drivers cuts cost as well. So there won't be an issue finding a job. The main topic will be finding the job/account that you want. You'll be a rookie and have to pay your dues, but this part of the process will be short-lived. With the proper work ethic, you'll have the opportunity for better jobs and accounts within no time.

The number one priority for trucking companies right now is to cut costs. While cost-cutting is always one of the top priorities for companies, it has become critically important in this current economic downturn. Freight rates have dropped because the amount of freight available has dropped, so carriers must cut back on costs to remain in business during times of decreasing revenues. One of the largest expenses for trucking companies is their payroll. By hiring students straight out of school instead of experienced drivers, the trucking companies are able to save a lot of money. So in this respect, the economic downturn is actually helping students find jobs!

In speaking with several trucking companies that own their own CDL driving schools, most of them are hiring as many student-drivers as they can get. A few of them had told me there was a temporary hiring freeze during December, but that was related more toward their end-of-year financial numbers than it was to demand. A slowdown or freeze in hiring in December is common across many industries. But even in these tough economic times, most trucking companies were not slowing down their hiring of student truck drivers.

High Turnover Prevents The Need For Layoffs

The trucking industry is famous for its incredibly high turnover rate, which tends to average over 100% for many companies. Because of this, if a trucking company wants to downsize its fleet, all they have to do is slow down their hiring for a short time and the fleet size will shrink from turnover alone. So for most companies, especially the larger trucking companies, there is never a need to layoff drivers.

So as you can see, even though times are tough in the economy and the media outlets love the word "layoffs" in their headlines, the trucking industry continues to bring in as many student drivers as ever to fill in the gaps caused by turnover and to keep the cost of labor down. So if you're considering a career in the trucking industry or are in the process of getting your CDL training, you likely have very little to be concerned about. Jobs are plentiful for new drivers in good times and in bad, and there are a lot of trucking companies that offer their own CDL driving schools that you should consider.

If you previously had a CDL and would like to get back into the industry, now is a perfect time to do so. For some people they may have been a trucker and then moved into a career and are now looking to move from that career into a job that allows them to travel and see the country. Increasingly men and women entering trucking school are not first, time truck drivers, but may be people retiring from another profession or coming back into trucking due to downsizing or layoffs at their current job. For these individuals it may be tempting to just do some brushing up on their own and then getting their CDL, but this is often a very costly mistake. There are several very good reasons why someone with an expired or lapsed CDL should complete a full truck driving program at a private or company sponsored school. By understanding why this is highly recommended by most in the industry you can decide if it is the right option for you in the profession.

DOT and FMCSA Requirements

Health Requirements:

To ensure the safety of all drivers and for the protection of other drivers on the road, the Department of Transportation and The Federal Motor

11

Carriers Association has certain minimum health requirements for all drivers. It's best to visit your doctor to ensure that you would be eligible to pass the minimum health requirements.

Vehicle Requirements:

To ensure the safety of your truck and for the protection of other vehicles, the Department of Transportation and The Federal Motor Carriers Association has certain minimum requirements before they will determine a truck is safe for operation.

Hours of Service

The Department of Transportation and The Federal Motor Carriers Association limits the amount of time you can work in a given day and week. Your time is divided into three primary sections:

On Duty Time — Time you are available for work and required to be on or near your truck.

Off Duty Time — Time you are allowed to rest and recover.

Driving Time — Time you are physically moving the truck

The guidelines are as follows:

11 hours of drive time per day

14 hours of on-duty time per day

10 consecutive hours of off duty time after 14 hours on duty

70 Hours of On-Duty time per week

34 consecutive hours of off duty time after 70 hours of On-Duty time

Disclaimer: this is a small overview of DOT and FMCSA requirements. Please take the proper precautions and do further research regarding DOT Hours of Service, Vehicle, and Health requirements to ensure that these rules adhered to. Severe penalties can incur if you do not follow these guidelines. You can visit www.FMCSA.org for further information.

Getting Up To Speed

There are a lot of changes in the trucking industry that happen regularly. This can include everything from regulations by the Federal Motor Carrier Administratio; to changes in the way that state reᵈuires accidents to be reported. Being up to date is essential obtaining your CDL and being able to get out on the road and have the confidence and competence to be able to handle situations as they arise. Some schools have "refresher" courses for people who are re-entering the industry. In addition you have been out of the trucking industry for a period of time and it does take a mental adjustment to get back into the swing of driving a truck. Having a chance to work through both the theory as taught in the classroom as well as the practical, hands-on experience will jump start your ability to pick up where you left off.

Learning New Technology

Trucking, just like every other industry, has changed in its use of technology. No longer are truckers out on the road on their own, they are in constant contact with dispatchers and managers at each mile that they drive. GPS fleet management systems can track everything from your speed to how long you were stopped, all in real time and all with amazing accuracy.

However, you should also learn about the technology that can help you to stay safe on the roads, including automatic systems that notify you when there are potential problems with the rig, ways to plan routes with safety in mind, apps and browser based programs that allow you to find loads and a range of other options designed to help you do your job.

Getting Rid Of Bad Habits

Over time all drivers develop bad habits, some which are not all that significant and some which are potentially problematic from a safety viewpoint. By being in truck driving school and being required to follow industry standard procedures you can get rid of the bad habits you had slipped into when you were driving before.

Having to go through routine pre-trip safety inspections, learning basic checks to perform on your rig and understanding the correct driving techniques will all help you to be more successful in returning to the profession. It is essential that you let old ways of doing things go and learn and practice new methods so you are driving just the way that employers want to meet all safety and insurance re uirements.

Furthermore, most STABLE trucking companies now require that drivers have completed a truck driving school program that is approved by their insurance carrier. This is because the liability and commercial vehicle and fleet insurance on the trucks and drivers is now a major part of their operating budget.

Insurance carriers provide discounted insurance for those drivers that have completed driving schools over those that have not. If you have an accident, even if it was years ago, this could be the difference between being considered for a job and not even getting a second glance.

Retuning to truck driving school if you have held a CDL before may seem like redundant training at first glance. However, in today's employment reality, it is often the most critical factor in landing that all important first job. Take your time, research the schools and choose one that has a great reputation with the trucking companies in your area.

Remember that trucking schools offer different schedules including intensive trainings over a few weeks or part-time trainings that may be several months to complete. This scheduling allows you to pick the school that works for you based on your current job and your ability to have the time to take the training.

One of the biggest hurdles to overcome when entering the trucking industry is the thought of being away from your friends and family. Or the idea of being in control of such a massive piece of equipment. I can still remember the first time that I was behind the wheel. It was overwhelming—all the gauges on the truck. I was having to shift gears, coming from someone who didn't even know how to drive a car with a stick shift—the people on the road. Having an instructor added to my nervousness as well.

Few people grow up dreaming of being a truck driver. Most have tried several other things before stumbling onto trucking. I consider trucking a sure-fire path to stability for the following reasons:

People will always need a reason to move something from point a to point b
. Trucking has a low barrier to entry, but many people don't have an acceptable

16

driving record to find a suitable job

, 64% of all freight is transported on a truck

. People who get into trucking don't stay long because of various personal

factors

.

Drivers can't maintain a good safety/driving record while driving.

Drivers are failing random drug and sobriety tests.

Driver jobs will be plentiful regardless of the economy.

People become professional driver for many reasons, some want to get paid as they travel but they understand that it is a job first so they are happy. Some choose trucking to escape a negative environment. That negative environment could be someone looking to reenter the workforce after a jail sentence. Trucking is one of the few well-paying industries that look past a person's criminal record. Many truckers were introduced to trucking at a young age by a father or uncle or grandfather and knew from an early age that they wanted to become a trucker driver. Some people become drivers simply to experience the adventure. Often, a person, will retire from another career such as military, or police officer and take a job as a driver.

Some become truckers because of the potential to make good money with a company that offers an excellent benefit package.

What are some things that should be taken into consideration before taking a truck driving job?

The candidate for the open road should be self reliant and responsible. He must be disciplined and dependable. Drivers need to be on time to pick up and deliver their loads. How else will goods show up on shelves when they are supposed to?

The right person means that the driver's family is on board with the potential life changes that his/her family will undergo. It is not a decision that the potential driver should make alone. Before taking a truck driving job there should be a serious discussion. With your partner.

You can't guarantee that you will make it back by certain dates or times to handle things. Yes, this also mean you can't guarantee that you will make it home for some of your kids important events. Relax, you won't miss all of the events if you plan ahead and keep your dispatcher clued in but you probably won't make them all.

Be sure you consider what it means to be away from home 2 or 3 weeks at a time before deciding you want to become a trucker. I always recommend that a person pretend he or she is gone away from the home for 3 weeks and let the spouse handle everything in the home just as she would if you were gone.

This will help insure you didn't forget to cover something before you leave away from home on the big road.

Many drivers get on the big road without asking enough questions about becoming a trucker. They don't realize how taxing it is on family life until they become truckers out on the road away from home for weeks. Most don't know that there are so many uncontrollable situations that can easily turns stressful. Stressors that include random breakdowns and unexpected detours. Some people become truckers before they realize that they would have to deal with four wheelers who seems to care little about safety on the highway or just don't understand. Drivers also find that it is expensive to be on the road if they don't plan ahead for being on the road. Continuously spending money in truck stops every day will eat up a paycheck. A paycheck that's already tough to live on because trucking has a huge learning curve and the pay scale for new drivers is extremely low. For this and many other reasons most drivers don't last long on the road before they leave to do an "easier" job. Trucking is a great industry, we need drivers out here who respect trucking. I say respect, because you don't have to love driving to be a truck driver; but you should respect how the industry can have a positive impact on your life.

You need to be good at budgeting and understanding exactly how you are paid. Too many drivers get angry because they feel they are being ripped off. Many are, but the biggest problem is they often do not fully understand how to maximize their pay. Even as a company driver you are really your own business man and you need to think like a business. Your dispatcher is your customer, You need to make him happy and try to cooperate. Plan ahead, let him know what your needs are days in advance. Don't wait until he gives you your next load to tell him you want to go home. But you also need to know when to say no. If they are under pressure to get a load delivered, but to do so means making you break a regulation such as hours of driving or some such, you can either agree or stand up and say no. Whatever you decide, you are the one who gets the ticket if you are caught. Worse yet if a fatal accident occurs while you are in violation of the Hours of Service, criminal charges can be bought against you. You can be arrested and serve serious jail time due to the incident.

Drug and Alcohol Testing

Trucking has zero-tolerance for any drug use or drinking alcohol before operating a vehicle. The Department of Transportation requires all drivers to have passed a drug screening and be in reasonably good health. Any failed drug test will make it nearly impossible to work for any reputable company for a minimum of 5 years. Some companies will hire you, but they're usually not the most reputable companies. If you consume alcohol, you need to make sure that you don't get behind the wheel of a vehicle for at least 12 hours. When driving a personal car, it depends on the state's legal limit on whether or not it results in a DUI. When driving a commercial vehicle, there is zero-tolerance for any alcohol consumption. A DUI conviction in a personal or commercial vehicle will result in termination of your employment and a five-year ban on working with any reputable company.

You'll be subject to random alcohol and drug testing as well.

If you feel that you may have a drug or alcohol problem, it's best to seek professional help BEFORE getting your CDL. Other than an accident, a failed drug or alcohol test is the quickest way to lose your CDL and ability to provide for your family.

Driving record

A satisfactory driving record is vital to obtaining and maintaining a CDL and being eligible for suitable employment. An appropriate driving record consists of the following items:

No more than one accident in the last 1-3 years

No more than one speeding ticket above 1-10 miles above the speed limit in the last 1-2 years

No speeding tickets above 10 miles per hour above the speed limit in the last 1-2   years

No reckless driving convictions in the last five years

No suspensions of your driving license (be prepared to give detailed explanations for any suspension of driver privileges)

No DUI/DWI convictions in the last five years

While this list may seem daunting, it's an indicator of job stability. Many drivers and potential drivers have problems obtaining and keeping their license do to these guidelines.

Good driving habits and having a good driving record is also one of the best forms of marketing for a trucker. Accidents, late deliveries, damaged goods and much more will all follow drivers on their records and potentially keep companies from getting new accounts for hauling freight. All companies have a risk assessment score, and the worse the score, the harder it is to get loads.

Good driving habits need to be practiced all the time, especially with truck drivers. In 2008 alone, there were 4,229 Fatalities in Crashes Involving Large Trucks. The nature of truck driving is a dangerous one to begin with, but when adding sleep depravity, exhaustion, distraction, weather conditions and or a number of other factors, the risks grow higher for truck drivers, other drivers and pedestrians.

How do you find the best truck driving job to suit you?

First remember the phrase, best truck driving job to suit you. There is no perfect job or trucking company. (Just like there is no perfect driver, yes me included!). Keep in mind, there are many types of truck driving jobs, ranging from dump trucks to heavy hauling and hauling anything in between.

There are several ways to research the best trucking companies.

They include but are not limited to:

Searches on Google and Youtube

Talking with family and friends in the industry

Joining Facebook Groups about the industry

Interviewing different companies

You can also try visiting your local truck stops and browse the brochures that companies place there. There are hundreds of trucking magazines and brochures there that lists companies and their profiles. These help you get a general idea of who to contact and use for comparison of benefits, wages, traffic lanes (this is the area that a carrier commonly travels). You will see that a lot of companies only hire in certain states or regions of the country.

After identifying a selection of companies you like, get your notepad call them and ask them questions like -

How often will you get home?

How many days will you get off when you do get home?

Ask about benefits that matter to you. (Companies have different insurance requirement, etc) Find out if they have a rider program if that is important to you. Not every company allows riders. A rider program allows spouses, children, friends, family members, and even pets to ride along on trips.

Ask about the pay structure, including how much you can expect the first year.

Truck driving provides a solid career path with lots of potential for growth. You can start as a company driver and gain the necessary experience at that level. You can go on to buy a truck or several trucks and lease on to a company or get your own authority. You could communicate with shippers to establish relationships while your driving so that you can eventually secure contracts for when you have your own trucking company. Side note: you can't solicit business while working with another company

Part 2 — Basic steps to obtaining your CDL

The truck driving school of your choice will guide you through the necessary steps to get your CDL. Their courses will give you the state-mandated education to get your foot in the door.

Online practice tests help you study for the Class A Commercial Driver's License so that you can legally operate semi-trucks and trailers. To do that, you need to pass a series of written CDL truck tests and receive the proper endorsements based on your goals and your choice of a trucking career that you have decided to pursue. The tests vary and include materials such as general knowledge about this license, combination vehicle tests, tests for hauling doubles and triples, HAZMAT endorsement, tanker, and other exams. All of these resources will assist you with your CDL training class.

If you wish to get a high paying truck driving job in the US, you need to obtain your CDL (Commercial Driver's License) for these vehicles.

The test includes various practice examples that test different aspects of your truck driving knowledge.

CDL License Tests, CDL Endorsements & Additional Information

We have provided all of the information to get your CDL license and qualify for a truck driver. As a job seeker, it is of paramount importance that you understand how this program works in detail and get your commercial driver's license (CDL). To obtain it, you need to review all of the sections of this test, including the following.

- **General Knowledge CDL Test** - Before signing up to take the CDL license and earning your commercial truck driving license, you need to test your general CDL knowledge through the CDL practice test.

- **Combination Vehicles Test** - Testing your knowledge of combination vehicles required before taking the CDL license test at the DMV.

- **Air Brakes Test And Skills** - Air brakes are a crucial component of every commercial vehicle, which is why you need to showcase your skills and take the state-certified test.

- **HAZMAT Endorsement** - If you want to advance your career, the HAZMAT endorsement is a great way to do that.

- **Tanker Endorsement** - The option of earning a tanker endorsement as part of the CDL license test is also beneficial for all truck drivers. Test your knowledge and identify the areas where you need improvement.

- **Doubles And Triples Endorsement** - Prepare for your doubles and triples endorsement by passing the practice test and set yourself up for truck driving success.

- **Pre Trip Inspection Engine Compartment** - The pre-trip inspection engine compartment is another crucial part of a CDL license exam - helping you check what you know.

Other Important Information For Your CDL License Exam

To pass your CDL exam, you need to review your state's CDL manual and all of the relevant information there. Make sure to study the latest version for your particular state through this document - which outlines aspects such as eligibility, requirements, and testing procedures.

In the CDL manual, you can also expect to see a CDL study guide that covers all information that is required to pass your CDL exam. You can find more information about the CDL licensing procedures by visiting your state's official license agency.

Part 3 — Surviving your first year

Advertisements for truck driving schools will lead you to believe it is possible to make a hundred thousand dollars in your first year of trucking. However, this is a typically not the case. In reality, there is only so much you can learn in a three week course, especially not how to properly drive a big rig. You will, though, learn everything that is necessary to obtain your Commercial Drivers License (CDL). Having your CDL is the start of your learning process and will put you on the path to becoming a successful truck driver. After obtaining your CDL you'll more than likely have to undergo a mentorship program with a major carrier. This program will be the training you need to actually start your career as a driver. Most long-haul truckers don't work a typical 5-day, 40-hour workweek. Many truckers work upwards of 70 hours a week and rarely feel the comfort of their home bed. One might think that 70 hours of driving per week is insane - and it is. No truck driver actually drives for

70 hours in a week. Included in those hours are other aspects of the job - loading, unloading, waiting between loads, truck repairs, securing loads and other aspects of the job that do not actually include driving. It is important to remember, however, that truck drivers typically get paid by the mile. So the more time spent driving equals more money in pay. When it comes to actual driving time, a typical trucker probably averages 50-60 hours per week. It is also important to understand that many of those hours are not at 65 miles per hour, either. You must factor in traffic jams and driving through cities and towns.

Ten tips for New Truck Drivers

1. Develop a friendly professional relationship with your driver management team: This team is your life line to loads, which in turn equals miles and miles directly affect your paycheck. A good professional relationship with your support team can be the most challenging part of the industry. Many drivers struggle with developing this significant relationship. You can't be a pushover, but you can't be a nuisance either. Always think of developing a win-win relationship with your dispatcher. At the very beginning, you'll pretty much do whatever loads they send your way. As you show your value by having a solid work ethic and commitment to the company, you'll eventually get better loads. Just focus on being a friendly professional driver, and over time everything should work itself out.

2. Make your own Food for the road

Eating on the road can be very expensive and cause health problems down the road. Truck stops are full of temptations that can take a hit on your wallet and waistline. It's best to plan and have healthy snacks and meal prep to avoid this problem. Keep, a steady diet plan, keep it light on the carbs for six days and treat yourself on the 7th. Exercise twice a day for 15 minutes, once before your shift and once during the mid day break. To avoid help avoid exhaustion and sleep depravity you should be consuming a proportional nutritious diet and exercising daily. Avoid over-eating carbohydrate heavy foods that could make you sleepy and have a cup of coffee ready to go when you need it.

3. Accept all loads sent your way: In the beginning refusing, a load can led to a bad impression. By accepting loads you show the company that you are dedicated; besides you never know what load is waiting when you get where you're going. In time you can use your discretion as to what loads are good for you. One exclusion to this is that you only accept loads that you can legally pick up or deliver. If picking up a load will cause you to violate any DOT regulations, politely refuse it.

4. Safety first. Always get out and look before backing up. Better to explain why your load was late than to explain why you hit something.

5. Love your Safety Department: Recognize that your company's safety department is always looking out for your best interest. The Safety Department unfortunately is viewed like a police officer. When you need an officer, you love them, when they tell you that you did something wrong they're horrible people. Always remember that your safety department has nothing to gain by your loss or failure. Your continued success and compliance is what they are most concerned with. They will always be in your corner!

6. Explore your Company: Every Company has different divisions that you are able to move through to improve your experience. Certain companies have a different division that require certain skills, this allows you to change divisions and gain more experience instead of changing jobs (the grass is not always greener on the other side). By doing this you show value and dedication to your new employer. It allows you to stay with your current company, maintain seniority and gain experience valuable to future endeavors.

7. Hard work really does payoff: Success is measured by what you put into your job. Do a mediocre job and you'll get a mediocre return. Strive for more and you'll get more. Your efforts never go unnoticed in the transportation industry. Every fleet manager, dispatcher, or terminal manager will go the extra mile for that driver that gives 110%. Operations always know whom they can count on for the important loads. Also there is the opportunity to possibly gain employment in the company's support team.

8. Get the Experience you Need: Most companies require you go Over the Road (OTR) for a minimum of 6 months to 2 years before obtaining a local job or the best routes. Part of this is because insurance for new drivers is costly. Also, driving OTR is the best way to gain experience driving the truck and budgeting your time. The major carriers want drivers as soon as they are professionally trained, and will give them the OTR experience they need to be successful. Remember; If the Wheels are Turning, YOU are Earning!

9. Be Prompt and on Time: Your timeliness will set the tone with you and your carrier, so always be on time always. It's always better to be an hour early than one minute late.   Late pickups and deliveries can cause your company to lose significant amounts of money or, worse yet, lose the contract with the shipper. Issues like bad weather and roads are out of the control of truck drivers, it's easy to check the conditions of roads and weather of your chosen route online through each states DOT.

10. Stay Alert: The most important task to do is to keep your eyes on the road. It can be easy to get distracted with roadside action, cell phones, the radio or just "stuff" in general. You're driving a very big machine that is capable of putting everyone and everything in its vicinity at risk. Purchase hands-free devices for your cell phone so that you will be able to talk and stay focused, as well as practice safe driving habits like not searching for items or texting. Distracted driving is a major offense in the trucking industry. Reducing risk for trucking is beneficial for all sides

of the trucking industry. With simple research and the practicing of good habits, risk can be reduced significantly in order to save time, money and lives.

Tips for finding the best trucking job:

Experienced truck drivers are in high demand with a lot of of companies. On average, one year of experience is required before finding the best employment, but two years of experience is optimal. This isn't always the case. I found my company right out of school, but the learning curve was steep. It took about nine months to get a hold of things. By the time I was at my two-year mark, I had become an owner-operator; I will talk about that later. For this section, the trick to finding a better job with better pay starts before you interview. It starts before you apply. It starts before you fill out an application.

There are a lot of openings, but few companies that are willing to pay a driver the top dollar for their time. However, if you're careful, and follow these steps, you'll be well on your way to making more money, being home more often, and getting better benefits for you and your family. These days, it's not just about your driving experience that will lead you to a better truck driving opportunity, it's a bigger professional picture that if you make sure to do some of these recommendations, you'll get the job that you've been working for, for so many miles. Take a second, you deserve to know:

1. Make Sure You Have A Job Now. Imagine you're the recruiter. Do you want to hire someone that doesn't have a job? Potential hires are "hotter" prospects when they're currently employed. This means the new company has to make a better offer to steal you away from your current employer. Plus, if you have a job now, you don't have to worry about going without a paycheck.

2. Get Your Work History Together. Most employers will require all necessary info regarding your previous three (3) employers - minimum. Most of them also require your previous three (3) years worth of employers. If you've had several jobs, you'll need to be able to provide the names of the employer and supervisor's as well as the phone number and addresses for all the companies. Yes, it's a chore to dig up, but it's worth it. Also, type it up or get it typed up so you have something professional to present to a new employer. This is one of the most overlooked aspects of truck driver jobs hunting.

3. Check Your DAC History. Your DAC driver history is a transportation company's way of checking your driving history before checking your MVR (motor vehicle report). It's a good idea to know what the recruiters see when they're looking up your info. Disputing your DAC can be a chore, just FYI, in the event something is incorrect. However, you knowing what's on there also means you don't go into a conversation or interview not knowing information, about yourself.

4. Check Your Personal Driving History. That's right, your personal driving history. It might show something different - could be good or bad - than what your DAC history or MVR shows. The best way to find all the info, and find it for FREE, is call your insurance company. The company that insures your personal vehicle has access to all of your info and can quickly and freely tell you all the info that's associated with you. Again, you knowing all the available info prepares you for any question you might be asked.

5. Make Sure Your CDL Is Current. Too many drivers try to find a job and realize that their CDL (commercial driver's license) is expired. Just how in the world is a trucking company supposed to hire a driver that does NOT have a current CDL? That's an impossible question that is asked but goes unanswered every day. This is something painfully obvious, but lots of to-be drivers don't have a current CDL.

6. Get Added CDL Endorsements. Yes, it's some extra cost, an extra test periodically, but high dollar freight takes a higher level of insurance which means the driver will be held to a higher standard of knowledge. Tanker drivers make more than van drivers

7. Don't Have Your CDL? If you're going to school or to get training to obtain your CDL, you need to be aware of all of your options. Some of the big companies actually have their own school, will train you a minimal expense, and guarantee you a job when you graduate. However, they do sometimes require you to drive for them for a certain

amount of time - which is fair - considering they footed the several thousand dollar bill of you obtaining your CDL. You might also go to an independent school or a lot of junior colleges have CDL training programs. You might have to get a loan or pay out of pocket, but you're on your own in terms of deciding you drive for in the coming months and years upon graduation.

8. Get Current on DOT and HOS Requirements - Both Federal and State. The federal regulations don't always exactly line up with the state regulations. You need to know the different rules of the road and rules of cartage for the freight, truck, time, speed of delivery with regards to the states you're traveling through because regulations can change just by crossing a state line. But, if you know this info in advance, you'll have a more successful driving career, because you'll know info other drivers don't. It might seem boring to research, but exceptionally helpful in a sticky situation.

9. Join Your State's Trucking Association. Every state has one and the dues are usually pretty reasonable. You can stay current on regulations while also learning the whos and whats of your state with regards to trucking. Again, this is info that you never know when it'll help you out. Also, if you get involved - even a little bit, you'll meet a lot of people with a lot of connections to the trucking industry, and that can ⊠uickly lead to better employment opportunities.

10. Be Extra Careful Driving. This is THE most obvious thing to keep in mind when trying to get a better trucking job. Think about it, safe drivers, with safe driving histories, get the best jobs. Why? They take their time, do what their asked, and do it without damaging cargo, equipment, or the company's name. You do that and you'll be the one getting the better pay, better home time, and bigger bonuses.

11. Do Some Research. You need to know what opportunities are out there. You need to know the names of the companies that are hiring. Go to your local truck stop and find some of the digest magazines, they're covered with advertisements. But if you really want to know all the trucking jobs info quickly, use the Internet. Go to a search engine and search for some companie's or find a site that lists lots of companies that are hiring truck drivers. You can contact them, read about them, or apply with them, all from the convenience of your home. Imagine if you got a list of trucking jobs offers to choose what's best, versus, having to call a company and settle for what they give you. Also, when you interview, get a haircut first, shave, and dress up a little. You only get one opportunity to make a first impression, so be sure to make a great one.

Yes, this is a bit detailed, but it's also truth. Pay attention to some details, some small things, and you'll get big rewards. I've worked in the trucking advertising industry for about eight years and these are just some of the general helpful hints that recruiters look for that drivers don't pick up on. If you'll cross all your I's and dot all your T's, you'll be sure to be rewarded—Best wishes to you in you trucking career.

SECTION II

I still remember driving with the trucking company I work with and driving, and a voice spoke to me a calm, quiet voice. I've always felt that when God speaks to you, its a calm, steady voice -- it's a whisper. The voice said Maurice; you've tried your hand at so many businesses jumping straight in without even thinking about it. Without doing research, just throwing money, time, and energy into the business often at a loss. Many of these businesses weren't in your core competency. And things were hard and didn't result in true financial benefit. Not consistent benefit that could support a lifestyle. But trucking comes easy to you. Very easy. Maybe THIS is the business in which you should dive headfirst. Later that week, the company offered a pay increase to owner-operators, a very significant boost for them. I thought to myself, Maurice, you're doing the same thing that owner-operators are making; if they can do it, you can do it. That "if they can do it, I can do it" mentality has been a mantra for me. That very next day, I contacted the owner-operator recruiter and asked about the process of getting my truck. I spoke to three other people.

1.) My driver leader — There are a lot of guys not making money because loads are to heavy and they have to reject loads

2.) the guy who trained me on intermodal (18 months back) — he said don't do it because the payments are too high and they'll take your truck if you leave the company

3.) and a guy who I trained on intermodal (12 months prior) — who got a truck six months after that and spent the next few months telling me to do it. This was refreshing because a lot of times, people don't motivate you to level up or improve your circumstances. He even said I'm making a killing, but with YOUR work ethic you'll be making a KILLING

So that Friday, I was talking to the owner-operator recruiter, and I was still hesitant, but she sold me on it and told me to stop working for peanuts. I signed the lease for the truck that day while I was with my oldest son (my only son at the time).

I remember being cautiously excited; I didn't even tell my girlfriend at the time. I didn't want to hear any discouraging words. I said to myself that I was going to wait until I got three checks before I told her. We already had a rocky relationship due to a bunch of factors. I was dealing with a divorce, a bad one at that, and dealing with issues seeing my oldest son because my ex was trying everything in her power to keep me from him. I had just caught traction as a company driver. Nine months prior, I had almost hit a breaking point and started looking for a "regular" job. I have a bachelor's degree, so finding a job making at least $40k would've been easy, which isn't enough money in 2019 for what I want out of life. And I'm sure that if you're reading this book that you want the most out of life. And in a lot of ways having more money helps with that.

Here are a few of my favorite lines about money from some of my favorite movies:

The Wolf of Wall Street — Leonardo Dicaprio — "Money is the best drug of them all! .. money gets you better food, better cars, and better pussy."

Wall Street 2: Money Never Sleeps — Michael Douglas — "Money is a bitch that never sleeps .. it watches you when your sleep and gets jealous."

I think I Love My Wife — Chris Rock's Manager — "You can lose a lot of money chasing women, but you won't lose any women chasing money."

I'm sure we'll have instances in our life where we either didn't have enough money, wanted more money, got treated differently because we didn't have money, or experienced better treatment because we did have money. So we know that money matters.

Luckily, right before I was about to give up on trucking at that eight-month mark, everything started to click. This brings me to a quote by Dennis Waitley— "Failure should be our teacher, not our undertaker. Failure is a delay, not defeat. It is a temporary detour, not a dead end. Failure is something we can avoid only by saying nothing, doing nothing, and being nothing."

This above image speaks volumes to me. Then comes the point in life where when you do keep hitting roadblocks, you start to get discouraged. This would've been me had I given up after eight months of trucking. Who knows where my life would've gone after that. The man in the top picture is determined, but look at the guy in the bottom picture he's defeated. Imagine him going home to a frustrated wife, an eviction notice, or hungry children. But through God's grace, I had just enough work ethic and determination to keep going, and things clicked, and the world of trucking truly opened up to me. Looking back on it, nine months isn't long at all. But at the time, I was scared.

I overcame that steep learning curve, and things started to stabilize.

After that first check, I was shocked at amazed I was making triple the money for doing the same work. I remember the song I used to play every Saturday morning when that direct deposit hit "Got a check" by Young Thug — don't judge me lol. It was life-altering money. It felt everything I went through in life prepared me for that moment. And this time, I was going to do what I was supposed to do with the money, which brings me to my best advice on trucking. Don't worry about if you're going to make money; as long as you have a work ethic, have the gift of gab, know when to speak up and know when to stand down, and work smart and hard; you're going to make some LIFE ALTERING money!

But three years later, I did the exact opposite of what I said I would do. I hired a few drivers -- 3 of three weren't worth a damn, one of them was very good, but he just bounced one day and ended coming back briefly and ended up working for someone else after a day. But there's one rock star on my team. We have an excellent working relationship. And have had very few hiccups and no heated discussions. That's why it's to make sure anyone you hire fits with your company culture. I had added three trucks, with a total of two trucks at the time of this writing.

I'm open about my number of trucks to let you know that you're not that far away from really changing your life. As I transition into other businesses and out of the driving role, I'll focus on growing the trucks and drivers and revenue. But I was just squandering money. I wasn't paying my taxes, and I wasn't saving any money. I was taking trips, going on dates, buying clothes, and giving the money away. It's easy to have $50+ in savings within two years. So I say this as a reverse role model. Everything else I talk about in this book, you should follow my lead. But when it comes to saving, investing, and paying your taxes.

Turn to a book written by an author of my publishing company that is an expert in those matters. Had I followed the proper steps, I would've achieved my goal of getting out of the driving role by 40. Yes, if you're reading this book, I don't expect you to drive for the next 10, 20, or even 30 years unless you want to. My goal is to teach you that trucking is a GREAT business. It's a tremendous cash-flowing business. And when you do what you're supposed to do with the money, you can grow your asset base in other companies, stocks, or real estate so that you can eventually stop trading your time for money. That's the journey I'm on now.

Here I am making more money than I've ever made in my life, but I haven't saved anything and haven't bought any assets outside of my trucks. I've grown tho. One reason for my lack of growth in that department is that while my income dramatically increased. I hadn't grown to be the type of person that can handle that kind of money. Anthony Robbins talks about BE — DO — HAVE.

Do you know what's worse than not making any money and being broke? Making money and STILL being broke!! Now you're just dumb and broke. That's what happened to me even though I made $1,345,000 in revenues with about $345,000 in net profit, BUT I have nothing to show for it. Well, I have the experience of wasting that kind of money. I have looked good in the outside world. But what I don't have is $1,010,267 in revenue with $303,080 in net profit. That's an additional $200,000 in revenues and an additional $33,000 in net profit. An additional $10,000 per year without putting any physical work in is phenomenal!!

"Profits are better than wages."
    - Jim Rohn

The crazy part about it is that recruiting is simple; it's not easy, but it's simple. Adding trucks to your fleet is just as simple. But before I dig into that, let's talk about getting your first truck, which is quite possibly the most critical decision that you'll make in your career. Your first truck can make you or break you. It's akin to the first woman you decide to marry. Any of you reading this book that has gone through a divorce or had a child with someone that you're no longer with should be able to relate. Divorce is expensive, and so is child support. My first truck was a lease-purchase through my employer. A lot of people are against lease purchasing because of the cost of your lease payments. But it's not a "cost"; it's an investment in trucking security. A GOOD lease purchase will have a kick-ass warranty attached to it and tons of steady freight to haul. That's so important and so vital to your success; that I have to repeat it.

A GOOD lease purchase will have a kick-ass warranty attached to it and tons of steady freight to haul. I still remember my first major repair on my first truck after about three months of making great money. I was about 20 minutes east of Galesburg, IL, and my turbo went out. The turbo is what gives your truck go, and it's a $3,000 - $6,000. I was frustrated, scared, and worried, but when I got the news that the warranty covered everything. I was relieved. I missed out on the revenue that I would've made that day, but other than that, things worked out perfectly. That brings me to an important point; to get a good back up truck as soon as you can. Because, as you know, if your wheels aren't turning, you aren't making money. A lease payment will be somewhere between $500 and $750 per week. Yes, per week!! But when you're with a company that gives you steady freight AND you have a solid work ethic that lease payment won't even phase you. This brings me back to the point that it's never whether or not you'll make money; it's about what you're going to with the money. Because no matter how much money you make. No matter how long the gravy train is. There will come a week or a month that the faucet will go from a full stream to a slight drip; you must have reserves for that moment so that you don't turn that minor inconvenience into a financial catastrophe in which you're not able to take care of your obligations.

If you don't remember anything else in this book, remember this trucking money will have you go from broke to thinking that an endless stream of money will drop into your bank account.

That's why you have to make the right purchase on your first truck. I say the first truck because while my first truck was a great purchase, my second truck was one of the worst investments in my life. I called her baby girl, and just like an older man dating a younger chick, she always had her hand out looking for money. In this case, the baby girl always needed something fixed. A week after buying her, my regen system went out, and it was a $10,000 repair.

And that was just the beginning that truck was always in the shop. I had the guts to add to my fleet. Which is essential; you have to take chances to grow. Every month she was in the shop for something. The truck also had the dreaded Volvo D13 motor, which had a factory defect with the injector cups. A huge key to success is taking the positive from every setback. The company I was with allowed me to take out a loan on that repair and I paid $583 per week until the $10,000 balance was paid. I'm going to break that down to help you understand just how much money I was making.

My truck payments, including payments on a loaner truck and fixed expenses before fuel, were $2,173 per week plus payroll for having one driver, and I was still bringing home well over $2,000 per week. Once that $10,000 loan was paid in full, I should've put that same $1,093 ($583 for the repair loan and $510 for loaner truck payments) into a savings or investment account to grow the business. It just dawned on me how much money I was burning. But that's why I want you the reader to learn from me. My work ethic is top-notch. I'm willing to bet that I'll run circles around most truck drivers. But my bottleneck is being a good steward with my finances. It's a constant struggle, but I'm learning from it.

Little did I know that I was about to be confronted with thousands of dollars of repairs per month from this one truck. While my first truck just kept on moving. Making a bad buy with a truck not only costs you money from the repairs, but there's also the downtime and the scrambling that I did to keep moving—getting loaners here and there—sharing another truck with my main driver. It just throws you off. I did know of a few people here and there that did luck up and got a sound truck for a low price, but for your FIRST truck, it needs to be something reliable. You simply can't afford the hiccups in the early stages.

That truck kept causing problems, and I kept sinking money into her. I did learn the lesson to — never buy a truck from a leasing company because those trucks are like buying a rental car. The drivers who drove them didn't care about the trucks. When you choose to grow, your feet find trucks that are for sale by a reputable dealer or had one or two owners. Pretty much the same concept of buying a car. My third truck purchase was RiRi, a 2007 pre-emissions Volvo with a D12 motor in it RIRI was a great buy. She's still running strong today. I did get into an accident in the truck, which was another moment of truth for me.

In the meantime, baby girl finally died on me, and the motor went out, and I sold her to the mechanic that fixed RiRi after her wreck.

On top of that, I would've added about a truck a year. Adding trucks has several benefits:

The more trucks you have, the more money you can make because when ONE truck breaks down, you're not stuck because you have one or two back up trucks. I can't stress this enough; trucking is a REVENUE driven business, not an EXPENSE driven business! Of course, you'd like to spend less on fuel. But fuel cost doesn't matter because you should either have fuel surcharge that offsets that. If you have an authority, you add that into your bid for the job of hauling the freight. Of course, you'd like to spend less on repairs ...but often we spend most of our repair budget. When one truck breaks down or has signs that something isn't quite right, you can put that truck into the shop and hop in your backup truck. Anyone that's ever owned a car, or been in a long term relationship, etc. understands that the key to keeping things moving is just to keep going. Money in trucking is about keeping your wheels turning.

You have first to BE the type of person that knows what to do with money, power, or whatever your long term goal is. I also was in another tumultuous relationship where I spent far too much time trying to fix the relationship than be on my purpose and grow my business. In trucking with minimal effort, you can go from driving to completely removing yourself from the driving role without affecting your income.

The less you work, the more your income should grow. You will unleash the power of OPT … Other People's Time.

Disclaimer the financial blueprint I'm giving is a lesson in reverse role modeling. I did not do what I was supposed to do with the windfall of money that came into my life after I became an owner-operator. It felt like I had a money tree. We learn from people in different ways. My biological father has been an example of a reverse role model in my life. He wasn't in my life at all, and I committed to myself that when I grew up that I would be in my children's lives. Once he got a teaching job, his only goal was to retire. He was famous for saying that once he retired that he wasn't going to do anything, and that's what he did for the last 12 years of life. I committed to a life of continuous learning and doing everything in my power to being able to live my life to the fullest extent until the day I take my last breath.

But back to trucking, remember when I said that the most critical question for an aspiring owner-operator isn't —

Will he make money or not?

The question that should be asked is —

What will I do with the money once I make it?

I'm assuming that you're going to follow the steps laid out in this book. Get a good truck with a warranty, and hopefully, that company will have a loaner program for when your truck breaks down. Have a strong work ethic. As an owner-operator, you'll have more autonomy because you're a boss, which is a gift and a curse. The gift is no one is telling you when to come to work and how long to come to work. The curse is no one is telling you when to work and how long to go to work. You have to have the self-discipline to set a goal for a particular dollar amount that you MUST make in revenues every day and commits to accomplishing that goal every day. And save a minimum of 10% of your income; NO MATTER WHAT! You really should be able to put up way more. The kind of money that you'll be making you could set aside 30 or 40% of your income. It's essential that you do this from the beginning and build sound habits in the beginning before your lifestyle catches up with your income. It's called Parkinson's Law - - expenses rise to meet income. I know what you're thinking. That's not going to be me. If I'm making that much money, saving it will be easy. I said that, and I know countless owner-operators that said the same thing as well. The money is going to come in droves and on a weekly or daily basis, and you'll eventually develop the mindset that it'll always be that way, and you can put money up next week. But next week never comes. You have to start TODAY! You must have reserves for the temporary setbacks you'll encounter in trucking. Save money towards repairs.

My company calls it a maintenance reserve where they set aside a certain amount (3 to 20 cents per mile) that go into a separate account for when you have repairs. Don't touch this account; it will come in handy when repairs come and instead of repairs coming from the new money you've made for that week or that month. It'll come from the account that was set aside for repairs. You'll be making more than enough money to enjoy an upgraded lifestyle AND put money to the side. You've also got put aside 10-20 % aside for taxes. If you've never been an independent contractor before your life is about to change. As a W2 employee, the IRS takes their money BEFORE you get your check. As a 1099 independent contractor, you get your money FIRST, and then you pay the IRS. Sounds exciting, doesn't it, but it can also be a recipe for disaster. Not filing and paying your taxes can have serious side effects on your life.

If you can follow these simple steps, not only will you life change but you'll be able to continue to grow onto bigger and better things:

1.) Get a solid and dependable truck

2.) Get with a company with a steady and reliable source of freight and offers a loaner

program for when your truck(s) breaks down

3.) Go to work every day with a goal for how much you need to make

 in revenue

4.) Save money for yourself, repairs and taxes

5.) Re-invest back into your business by buying trucks and hiring drivers

6.) Properly maintain those trucks

7.) Take care of your drivers

8.) Get from behind the wheel and build your business

I struggle with steps #4 and #5; I haven't reached the ultimate success of step #8.

Writing this book has been a game-changer for me; I have set that goal to get from behind the wheel. Countless truckers have stepped away and no longer drive and have a steady stream of income from drivers that work for them and a base of trucks that can help you invest in other businesses or whatever goals they may have. But we're taking this journey together. Iron sharpens iron. Hopefully, this book will inspire you, and writing this book has inspired me.

I've done everything else on this list but like with any system. Forgetting any steps along the way will not allow you to reap the full benefits of the system.

OPT is a game-changer.

Have you ever bought a scratch-off lottery ticket and flipped $1 into $2 or gotten a free ticket with the chance to play another ticket?

Have you ever owned rental property and received a rent check in the mail? Instead of paying bills on the first, now someone is paying YOU on the first!

Once you received money that you didn't expend any physical labor, you'll never be the same!

Once you're on vacation and you see loads being picked up and delivered you'll never be the same

Once you forced to take a day off because you're sick or have to go to court or a truck breakdown keeps you from working, AND you still make money .... your life will never be the same.

Would you ever bet $24 to gain $1? Of course not, but that's precisely what you're doing when you trade your time for money. Think of all the things you've missed out on because you HAD to work .. think of your kid's game that you wanted to go to, but your HAD to work .... your best friends event but you HAD to work .... your significant other wanting to just lay in bed and spend time with you but you HAD to work ... if you're in a cold climate and the weather is brutally cold, but you HAVE to work ... it sucks!!

That's what happens when you work for money, that's YTFM .. your time for money. Life comes at you fast — it just dawned on me a couple of days ago that I've been driving for going on six years. While I've made strides in these last six years, there's a lot of things that I left on the table. Money that should've been put to its highest and best use. The positive about all this is that I have bigger problems today than I did six years ago, instead of asking myself how I am going to make ends meet. I'm asking myself how I can better utilize this disposable income. I'm a serial entrepreneur. Since fourth grade, I knew that I wanted to go into business for myself. The freedom that entrepreneurship affords you is priceless. I've tried and failed at countless companies. I'm sure that trucking isn't your first business, but I'm willing to bet that it's going to be the one that provides you with the most consistent revenue stream. Also, the most consistent return on your time and money invested. Trucking should be the platform that allows you to eventually invest in other businesses while remembering that trucking is the golden goose. When you're fortunate enough to find another golden goose while still growing your trucking business, that's when life will open up for you. I'm a firm believer that money attracts more money.

As in the parable of the talents in the bible in Matthew 25:14–30 tells of a master who was leaving his house to travel, and, before leaving, entrusted his property to his servants. According to the abilities of each man, one servant received five talents, the second servant received two talents, and the third servant got one talent. The property entrusted to the three servants was worth eight talents, where a talent was a significant amount of money. Upon returning home, after a long absence, the master asks his three servants for an account of the talents he entrusted to them.

The first and the second servants explain that they each put their talents to work, and have doubled the value of the property with which they were entrusted; each servant was rewarded:

His master said to him, 'Well done, good and faithful servant. You have been faithful over a little; I will set you over much. Enter into the joy of your master.'

— Matthew 25:23, <u>New English Translation</u>

The third servant, however, had merely hidden his talent, had buried it in the ground, and was punished by his master:

"Then the one who had received the one talent came and said, 'Sir, I knew that you were a hard man, harvesting where you did not sow, and gathering where you did not scatter seed, so I was afraid, and I went and hid your talent in the ground. See, you have what is yours.' But his master answered, 'Evil and lazy servant! So you knew that I harvest where I didn't sow and gather where I didn't scatter? Then you should have deposited my money with the bankers, and on my return, I would have received my money back with interest!

Therefore take the talent from him and give it to the one who has ten. For the one who has will be given more, and he will have more than enough. But the one who does not have, even what he has will be taken from him. And throw that worthless slave into the outer darkness, where there will be weeping and gnashing of teeth.'"

— Matthew 25:24–30, <u>New English Translation</u>

I've been that third servant many times in my life. While I didn't bury my money, I did spend it frivolously. I did invest it foolishly. As the saying goes, a fool and his money are soon parted. Commit to yourself today that when you start making real money in trucking. That you will be responsible for this newfound money, and you will invest it wisely.

As it says in the Richest Man In Babylon by George S. Clausen — Every dollar is a slave that should go to work for you. When you spend a dollar foolishly, you kill that slave and all the children of that slave, which would have also become your slaves. So it's not just about the money that you make in trucking. It's the additional revenue streams that you can create from your trucking profits.

It's also essential to start an LLC for your trucking company. Disclaimer: I am not a lawyer, and information in this book is not to be seen as legal advice. An LLC is the cooperate structure that I should've used because it would've kept me from being taxed at the corporate level and a personal level, known as double taxation.

That simple mistake has cost me about $30,000 over the last few years.

An LLC also protects you in case of an accident or catastrophic event causes a lawsuit. For example, if you or one of your drivers causes a multi-car pile up. In instances like these, lawyers target passenger car drivers to try and take down the big money trucking companies. The LLC protects your assets from being susceptible to a lawsuit.

To keep costs down but get an in-depth answer as to what corporate structure works best for you. Start a pre-paid legal membership that allows you to consult with lawyers for around $30 per month. After you get the answers to your questions, you can use a company like Legal Zoom to handle the paperwork.

You'll also need an EIN or Federal Tax ID number for your company. Which acts as the social security number for your business. This can be done for free, by going to the IRS website at:

https://www.irs.gov/businesses/small-businesses-self-employed/apply-for-an-employer-identification-number-ein-online

Many companies will try and charge you for this, but it can be done for FREE.

Get a business banking account. You'll need your EIN. You're articles of incorporation which will be prepared for you by your attorney or a company like Legal Zoom. This will allow you to start building credibility for your company. There are a lot of sources for building business credit, but the author doesn't have any personal experience in the matter. Make all your purchases for the business with your business debit card or checking account information.

Use this account to re-invest in the business; so that it can grow over time. Saving and re-investing 20% of your companies' profits will allow you to grow a business one truck at a time. One word of caution; be very careful not to get any NSF (insufficient funds or return check) fees on your account. When it comes time for funding, lending companies frown upon that. They see it as an inability to manage cash flow.

Keep track of your spending through a spreadsheet or bookkeeper. It's essential to start your business out the right way to build a strong foundation.

Hire a payroll company to pay you and any employees or independent contractors. It'll help you look more established.

In conclusion,

Becoming an owner-operator was truly a life-altering move for myself and my family. I urge you the reader to talk with other owner-operators about their experiences in the field. Be careful of that naysayer who find excuses outside of themselves as to why their business may not be as lucrative as they like. Yes, this is NOT a guaranteed path to success. For those who are willing to work and have sound people skills, this business will improve the lives of you and your family. Further down the line as you grow your business and re-investing the profits of the business. You'll be on the path to the next level by Obtaining Your Trucking Authority.

When leaping from owner-operator to starting your authority, most of your day to day operations will remain the same. Still, there is also a lot of new responsibilities that your carrier handled for you, such as:

DOT Audits — an audit performed by the Department of Transportation to ensure that all your paperwork and files are in order!

Here are the basic steps (some of these steps are similar to becoming an owner-operator):

Determine what type of legal company you would like to operate.

Do you want to work as a sole proprietor, as a corporation, LLC etc. If you are going to operate as a corporation then you will need to file articles of incorporation in the state where you intend to operate from.

You will need to either purchase or lease a truck and trailer. There are benefits to purchasing or leasing depending on your financial condition and what paperwork you desire to be responsible for during the year.

File for your authority and other Federal requirements depending on your specific operations.

Next, you will need to have your license plates for the states that you intend to drive through.

You'll need IFTA stickers for fuel taxes.

Purchase your insurance as required by the FMCSA.

Apply and obtain any state permits depending on your specific operations.

Put together your driver information and requirements as outlined by the FMCSA.

Receive your authority and permits.

Start hauling your own for-hire loads.

The steps can be complicated based on your particular operations and I recommend that you find a creditable trucking authority service that can assist you in determining all your specific needs and making the appropriate filings with the Federal Government and individual States where required and if possible handle your insurance as well. They can be found on the web by searching for keywords such as "Trucking Authority Service". The process can take as long as 30-45 days depending on your particular requirements. There are steps in the process that can be expedited but often the process will bog down with individual state filings.

Types of Trucking Authorities

Many times the ⓠuestion arises as to what are the various trucking authoritie's available. The right choice can make the difference in the amount of money you can earn. The following is a brief description of definitions used by the Federal Motor Carrier Safety Administration.

There are a total of eight different authorities that you could apply for. You could obtain only one or all eight or a combination thereof. Of course, this is determined partially by whether or not you are going to have any trucks owned or leased. Having your own motor carrier authority gives you the opportunity to have owner-operators lease to your authority. Having your own broker authority gives you the opportunity to handle loads in excess of your own requirements through the utilization of other authorized motor carriers.

MOTOR CARRIER: A company that provides truck transportation. There are two types of motor carriers, private carrier's and for-hire carriers. To operate as an interstate motor carrier, you must operate as either a private or a for-hire carrier.

PRIVATE CARRIER: A company that provides truck transportation of its own cargo, usually as a part of a business that produces, uses, sells and/or buys the cargo being hauled.

FOR-HIRE CARRIER: A company that provides truck transportation of cargo belonging to others and is paid for doing so. To operate as an interstate for-hire carrier, a company must also register with FMCSA. There are two types of for-hire carriers, common carriers and contract carriers. A for-hire carrier may be both a common and a contract carrier, but must file separate registrations to obtain both licenses.

COMMON CARRIER: Before January 1, 1996, this was a company that provided for-hire truck transportation to the general public. The services offered and the prices charged were published in a public tariff and these were the only prices the common carrier could charge.

CONTRACT CARRIER: Before January 1, 1996, this was a company that provided for-hire truck transportation to specific, individual shippers based upon private contracts between the carrier and each shipper, stipulating the services offered and the prices charged to each.

SELECTING "COMMON" OR "CONTRACT": The historical difference between these two types is reflected in the definitions immediately above. The ICC Termination Act of 1995 defines contract carriage as truck transportation provided under a contract, but, effective January 1, 1996, it no longer distinguishes between common or contract carriers. However, the Act specifically authorizes FMCSA to continue registering applicants as either common or contract carriers. The current principal distinction between the two types is that common carrier applicants must file proof of cargo insurance while contract carrier applicants are not re 🞏uired to do so.

FREIGHT FORWARDER: A company that arranges for the truck transportation of cargo belonging to others, utilizing for-hire carrier's to provide the actual truck transportation. The forwarder does assume responsibility for the cargo from origin to destination and usually does take possession of the cargo at some point during the transportation.

Forwarders typically assemble and consolidate less-than-truckload (LTL) shipments into truckload shipments at origin, and disassemble and deliver LTL shipments at destination. Forwarders must register with FMCSA. (Freight forwarders are not brokers.)

BROKER: Also a company that arranges for the truck transportation of cargo belonging to others, utilizing for-hire carriers to provide the actual truck transportation. However, the broker does not assume responsibility for the cargo and usually does not take possession of the cargo. Broker's must register with FMCSA. Another basic difference is that brokers arrange for truckload transportation whereby Freight Forwarders arrange for the transportation of less-than-truckload (LTL) shipments. (Brokers are not freight forwarders.)

GENERAL FREIGHT OR HOUSEHOLD GOODS (HHG) MOTOR CARRIER: After determining what type of authority you will need, now you will need to determine what you are going to transport. General freight includes everything except for household goods. Additional certification is reꟼuired for HHG movers as you must now certify that you are fit, willing and able to provide the specialized services necessary to transport household goods. And, that you will offer arbitration as a means of settling loss and damage disputes on collect-on-delivery shipments. And, that the operation will serve a useful public purpose responsive to a public demand or need.

BROKER OF HOUSEHOLD GOODS (HHG): You must certify that you are fit, willing and able to provide household goods brokerage operations and to comply with all pertinent statutory and regulatory re️uirements. And, that the involved services will be consistent with the public interest and the transportation policy.

BROKER SCHOOL: A good broker school could be an asset to you. Taking time to attend a one or two week ️uality broker school could be well worth the time and money spent. If interested,

WHAT IS THE BEST AUTHORITY TO GET? If you have your own trucks or plan to lease trucks, the absolute best to have is motor carrier and broker authorities for the reasons stated above.

Obtaining the proper insurance

Truck drivers must have proper insurance to drive heavy trucks on the highways. When they work for a trucking company the company takes care of the insurance re️uirements. Drivers who take the leap to become owner/operator truck drivers or small fleet owners become responsible for their own insurance. At that point they must be very knowledgeable about the type of coverage they need. They should discuss various options with insurance agents to determine the type of coverage and the proper amount of insurance re️uired to cover the needs of their new business.

Truck drivers typically begin their trucking careers working for a trucking company. Usually, the next step driver's sometimes take from working as hired drivers for trucking companies is to become owner/operators. They become business owners and purchase or lease their own trucks, trailers and equipment. As opposed to being hired employees, they hire themselves out to other trucking companies to haul freight for them. Choosing to become an owner/operator puts these drivers in control of the loads they haul. It also puts them in control of where they choose to go. Additionally, it allows them to earn more income.

Typically, after working for some time as owner/operators many drivers decide to take the next leap and become small fleet owners. They can start with one or several trucks. They can choose to hire other truck drivers or owner/operators. They could also decide to be the sole driver for their company.

The trucking industry is a highly competitive industry so new owners must have a plan to ensure their success. New trucking company owners must make decisions as to the type of freight they desire to haul and obtain the proper equipment. This could include dry van trailers, flatbed trailers, refrigerated trailers, etc. They also will need to decide if they plan to hire other drivers. These and other factors will determine the type of insurance their business requires.

Regardless of whether drivers decide to become owner/operators or small fleet owners they will be responsible providing all or part of the insurance for their truck, trailer and other equipment. Owner/Operators may have part of their insurance such as primary liability insurance covered through the company they are leased to. However, they may need additional insurance to cover their truck, plus any other equipment they have. Small fleet owners are entirely responsible for the insurance needs of their company.

Insurance options will need to be carefully considered. First and foremost is liability insurance. Federal law reuires truckers to have liability insurance to drive on the road. Primary liability insurance is the insurance which protects others on the road. Primary liability insurance protects the financial costs of the victims of accidents such as large medical bills, injury benefits, death benefits and damages done to the other vehicles involved in the accidents caused by you or one of your drivers.

Cargo insurance is the insurance which covers the loss of freight that is in the care, control and custody of the carrier.

From the time the gate is closed on the back of your cargo, you are responsible for the contents of your delivery until the final drop off at your destination. Your liability for cargo as the truck driver increases due to many factors like the distance of the journey, kinds of roads being traveled on, the value of the cargo and driver history. Each delivery will have its ad hoc circumstances involved with the final price of pay and coverage.

For your trucking company, the best kind of marketing that you can have is a good insurance policy. Clients need to know that the drivers they hire to transport their products will do so with proficiency and careful consideration. Following these tips can help ensure your clients that they can trust you to get the job done right before you're even hired.

It's not a shot at the drivers, but in a business deal like this, companies are going to be more interested in the cargo than they will the driver. Even though the safety of the two go hand in hand, if something is to happen to one or both of them, then the expense for the client will be at the cost of lost merchandise, not the driver.

The first way to reduce trucking risks that come with transporting cargo is to understand the cargo you're taking. What kind of cargo is it? How valuable is it? Are there hazardous materials involved? Does it need to avoid certain kinds of weather conditions? Is there an expiration date on them? By understanding the nature of the cargo being delivered, all of the proper permits, certifications and other preparations can be obtained in turn allow drivers to adjust operations for the job.

Truckers are required by the federal government to have at least a $750,000 coverage minimum for carrying regular cargo. However, if truckers are carrying hazardous cargo, they need to look into getting a much higher coverage policy which could range up to $5,000,000.

If you're not sure what circumstances cause more risk? Speak with your trucking insurance representative who will be able to help with exactly what permits, authority and or coverage minimums you should get.

You are having the proper insurance in place for your business enables you to financially protect your business—You may require extra coverage in addition to liability and cargo insurance. Your insurance agent should advise you accordingly. Take the time to choose your coverage wisely.

Trucking business 7-figure trucking. A million dollars in annual revenues only takes about three trucks. Once you have experience in the fundamentals of the business, you'll be able to grow this business and start or buy other companies as well.

I'll leave the reader with a handful of books to help further your journey:

Rich Dad, Poor Dad — Robert Kiyosaki

The Cashflow Quadrant — Robert Kiyosaki

The Richest Man in Babylon — George S Clausen

Think and Grow Rich — Napoleon Hill

The Art of Not Giving a F*ck — Mark Manson

The 5 Second Rule — Mel Robbins

Become a Youtube junkie — subscribe to their premium service and a world of educational videos about any topic that you can think of will open up to you.

Join our community at 6figuretrucking.com for more ways to grow your business and grow as a person. Feel free to email me at msanders@6figuretrucking.com

When you're ready for the big leagues, you progress your career forward from being an owner-operator and contracting with a major carrier to becoming the carrier. With your authority, you take your payments directly from the shipper, which means you get a bigger piece of the pie. Of course, with greater reward comes greater responsibility. You're responsible for finding freight, negotiating with brokers and shippers, and keeping paperwork organized and ready for the proper filing with the federal government.

SECTION III

Chapter 1: Pros & Cons Of Owning A Trucking Company

Owning a trucking authority can a lucrative endeavor, as opposed to working with a large trucking company. Nevertheless, truckers should understand that there's a lot of hard work and responsibility that goes into owning and operating your authority. The process of deciding to move away from a large company should be given major consideration; before any action is taken. Weigh your options and take note of the pros and cons, making such a decision.

Pros of becoming a Authorities

The trucking business is enjoyable and profitable. But it shouldn't be expected to be easy. To starting a trucking authority, one must put a lot of effort and hard work and money into it.

What Are The Pros Of Starting a trucking authority?

There are Advantages of starting a trucking authority. Independent drivers have plenty of positive things in their business; don't forget that these good things require an enormous amount of hard work and investments.

You are Independent

Owning a trucking authority means the freedom to make your own decisions. You decide who to work with, what loads to carry, and how much time to work. Your work and life only controlled by you.

Flexible Schedule

When It comes to your independence, You're free to plan your work and your working days/hours.

Great Income

Trucking authorities earn a lot more than owner-operators. They have a bigger revenue percentage for each load they haul. As a trucking authority, you control almost every aspect of shipment, and you earn more profit from it.

Family Time

While you plan your schedule, you can decide how much time to spend at work and at home. Trucking authoritys, in general, have more than enough time to spend at home with their family.

More Job Opportunities

Due to the driver shortage, skillful and experienced drivers are always welcome at any trucking company. So when you are looking for a driver, you don't have to spend a lot of time finding one.

Travel the Country and Get Paid for That

Being a truck driver is an adventure, especially if you are an OTR trucker. We're all down with seeing new things, and when you drive across the U.S., you'll see a bunch of exciting and fascinating scenery.

Freedom

Authorities have more room to decide on what loads to haul, who to work with, organizes his/her own business. Hence, taking time off is a personal decision with no confirmation needed from a company. Such autonomy has many advantages.

Flexibility

Along with being complete autonomy, owners can be flexible and work on their terms. You won't have to worry about the situation of the trucks because they're all yours. You get to make your schedule, which is great. Though you will still have to somewhat manage your time around the demands of the shipments, Authorities are dependent on themselves to get things done and therefore have the flexibility to run their business the way they want.

Profitability

As an authority, there is a greater potential to make more money with tax advantages and lower rates more than truck drivers working under a company because they claim a much larger share of the profits from each load. By owning the truck, owners get to control every part truck driving responsibility and therefore collect the profit for themselves.

Cons of Becoming an Owner

While owning a truck authority as it's pros, which maybe all fun and rosy, Do not think that being an trucking authority is easy. Truck Drivers fave many obstacles which can be overwhelming due to lack of experience and wrong expectations. If you are considering starting a trucking authority you have to be aware of the cons of this business.

Start-up Investment

Like every other business, starting a trucking authority requires start-up costs. Luckily for drivers, there's a lot of options to

77

start with. You can decide to go for a small truck or a van, or you can want to play big and start with your fleet of a few units right away.

Time

Running an authority brings autonomy, and you can take time off whenever you want, but a lot of your free time will require maintenance of your truck/fleet and keeping business records. If you think trucking authorities have a lot of spare time, you are wrong. You'll spend a lot of time paying your bills and maintaining your truck because nobody would do it for you, at least for free Owners work even more than company truck drivers because they have a lot more of the workload to cover on their own. From maintaining the truck to setting up contracts, owners don't have much downtime.

Stress

In the process of looking for trusted business partners and building a good reputation, the driver will face a lot of pressure. You will have to learn how to shuffle between administrative tasks, getting loads, and maintaining your truck so that your business will run smoothly. The pressure and stress faced by owners are greater than that of an owner-operator. One needs to research and network with trucking companies to find who pays the best and be consistent. It's not easy to leave one job for another due to contracts. Until one has established a good reputation in the industry and is getting loads regularly, starting an authority can be very stressful.

Start-up Costs

It can be really expensive, starting up a trucking company. But there are financing options, especially in the transportation industry. So although it can be expensive, there are options for you to become your own boss.

Insurance and All Registrations Are On You

Trucking authorities must get their insurance, DOT number, and many other documents to operate properly.

Taxes

Also You will have to pay your own taxes. However, you can find a specialist who can be in charge of it for you for a small fee.

Chapter 2: Steps For Starting Your Authority

Whether you are a professional driver or a rookie, here are the steps that you will need to take to get on the road with your own operating authority.

1 Develop a business plan

Before you start your business, make sure you have a business plan. It should show clearly what your revenue and expenses will be. Remember, all your expenses need to involve the money that you will pay yourself for living expenses. You may want to hire a business advisor to help you determine the plan that makes the most sense for you.

2. Determine what kind of business structure is best for you.

structures of trucking business include:
•Sole proprietorship
•Partnership
•Limited liability corporation (LLC)
•Corporation (C-corp, S-corp, etc.)

Each structure has advantages and disadvantages based mostly on liability and taxes. You may want to get an accountant to find out which structure best suits you and your business.

3. Save up money to cover start-up expenses

Starting a trucking business requires a large investment to be able to purchase a truck and get licensing requirements and registration. Identify sources for financing and secure a line of credit. Professionals recommend having enough money saved to cover your first six months of operation, including your lease payments.

4. Plan your business operations

Plan out how you want your business to operate, to avoid important issues like:

•Where will you park the truck/equipment?

•Who will maintain it?

•How will you find loads?

•How invoicing, accounting, payroll, and taxes will be handled

5. Comply with federal and state government regulations

Before you start operation, your company will need to comply with the following agencies:

•USDOT Number – The U.S. Department of Transportation (DOT) requires carriers to have an identifier that is used to collect and monitor safety information.

•Operating Authority carriers must receive operating authority from the DOT. This tells what kind of cargo you can carry.

•Heavy Vehicle Use Tax – To fund highway programs, the federal government will charge an annual tax on trucks that exceeds 55,000 pounds.

•International Registration Plan (IRP) - IRP distributes registration fees based on distance traveled in each state or Canadian province.

•International Fuel Tax Agreement (IFTA) –

•BOC-3 Filing

•DAT Authority will help you get your authority, handle your IFTA tax reporting, and help with other compliance requirements.

6. Obtain Insurance

Insurance is an important expense for trucking businesses. The Types of insurance needed for transporting freight include:

•Primary liability: $750,000 in primary liability coverage is needed to cover damage or injury done in case there's an accident, and you are at fault.

•Cargo: $100,000 is the amount needed to cover cargo, but this will depend on what you are hauling. Which covers damage to freight or theft.

7. Buy or lease a truck and trailer

When it comes to vehicles, you either purchase or lease equipment. Whichever way, you must first decide what type of freight you plan to hauling. Whether you plan on only running day trips, or will you need a sleeper cabin? Will your first vehicle be a van, or a trailer? Below are some of the types of leases:

•Operating Lease: this lease allows you to take care of maintenance, taxes and permits, and at the end of the lease you are allowed to walk away.

•Terminal Rental Adjustment Clause (TRAC) Lease: With this lease you can make a small down payment and at the end of the lease you can purchase the truck, or you can go for the leasing company to sell the truck.

•Lease Purchase Plans: Lease-purchase plans are primarily for truckers who don't have enough for a down payment or have bad credit. Experts say you typically pay more in such arrangements versus traditional financing.

8. Register Your Business with the appropriate State or County

This registration will have to be done based on the state you plan to operate. You will have to choose a business structure for your trucking business. Whether you operate a sole-proprietorship; or choose to limit your liability to the assets within the company. You will need to fill out and submit the necessary forms at the Secretary of State's office. These forms can be filled online and submitted once done. Complete and retain the proper documentation; because you'll eventually need that information for possible DOT audits.

9. Obtain an Employer Identification Number (EIN)

If you are an LLC, you must have an EIN number issued by the IRS. It is necessary for any individual that is also operating as a sole proprietor to also obtain an EIN to protect their privacy. Incase the EIN is absent, the driver must use their social security number (SSN) which can open them up to identity theft.

10. Register Your Business with the U.S. Department of Transportation

To start up a trucking business, you'll need to get United States Department of Transportation USDOT and Motor Carrier operating authority Number, or MC Number, from the Federal Motor Carrier Safety Administration (FMCSA). This USDOT number is what allows you to access all of your company vehicle, cargo, safety, and compliance information.

When you start the registration processes, there are some things that you need to know about your trucking company.

1. Where and how will you be operating?
2. The type of vehicle

3. Types of materials to be hauled
4. Weight of your vehicles?
5. Will you be hauling exempt cargo?
6. Are you going to be a freight forwarder or a broker?

This information will be filed under your USDOT number and will be available to any shippers you haul for. You will be given a PIN along with your USDOT number. This PIN is for any changes you make with the USDOT or FMCSA in the future. You will need to renew your USDOT number every two years, or anytime any changes are made to any of your information.

11. Apply for a Motor Carrier Number (MC#) with the FMCSA

Your Motor carrier number is what will give you the authority to participate in Interstate Commerce. All of the information you gathered for the USDOT registration will be needed to complete your application. You will be given your Motor Carrier Number immediately. Once your MC is issued, you'll have 20 days to complete the next two steps. Once those two items are on file with the FMCSA, your authority will become active within approximately 2-3 weeks. It will take another two weeks for you to receive your Authority certificate in the mail. You are not allowed to participate in Interstate Commerce until your motor carrier number is active.

12.Obtain Insurance

A truck driver is required to obtain Liability and Cargo insurance. FMCSA requires a driver to have at least $750,000 primary liability and $100,000 in cargo. The Insurance provider must report your coverages to the FMCSA for your authority to be active. If you make any changes to your Motor carrier number information, you must also report that to your insurance company and have them resubmit the information to the FMCSA or your risk having your authority go inactive.

13. Set up your International Registration Plan (IRP)

IRP is a process of registering a large number of vehicles if you're to operate in two or more areas. If you are operating a truck in multiple areas, you must yearly report mileage driven in each state and pay taxes on the mileage driven. This registration, you will need all the details about your trucks, including VIN, title information, purchase cost and date, as well as make, model, etc.

14. Set up an IFTA Account

The International Fuel Tax Agreement (IFTA) is an agreement among the lower 48 states of the United States that simplifies the reporting of fuel use by motor operators that travel in more than one area. Drivers with IFTA receive an IFTA license and two decals for each vehicle it operates.

15. Unified Carrier Registration (UCR)

The Unified Carrier Registration (UCR) Program allows individuals and companies who operate commercial motor vehicles interstate or international to register their business within the state they live and pay an annual fee based on the size of their fleet. Including any commercial vehicle carrying their goods and products across state lines, which includes carriers transporting intrastate goods.

16. Simple Permits

If you plan to haul in any state, you may need to obtain permits if you meet the state's criteria.

Chapter3: Finding Freight

If you're an authority who is trying to find the best load board for truck, or a fleet owner trying to learn how to get freight contracts, all Authorities are on the same trail. Here are some ways to find more loads. So If you've already started running your own trucking company and you find yourself stuck at deciding which freight is best for you, it is best to find the work that is worth your time. Finding freight is now so easy, thanks to technology. There are now resources all over that an help you grow your business. However, without proper planning, the path to go through can be unclear and overwhelming. So how do you succeed in as a trucking company? Find out below!

Learn about the Loads

Load boards allow carriers to search for loads using specific criteria. Enter your information – such as your truck type, pick-up date and location, and full or partial load. The load board then populates a list of matching, available loads.

What are you legally able to haul?

Pay attention to weight limits. Does the load's weight require a special permit? Heavier loads also use more fuel. Does the freight rate make sense for the weight/distance of the load?

Will you make money on the load?

Know your operating cost. It is the backbone of your entire business. You're taking money out of your own pocket by accepting a load that pays you less than it costs to run your truck. Be aware of deadhead miles and assessorial fees. Where is the drop-off location? If you are driving into a location known for having high fees (lumpers, tolls, long detention times, etc.), make sure the freight rate is enough to cover them and your cost of operation.

Is it a good rate for the lane?

Compare the freight rates to the average spot rates. Most load boards offer spot rate averages on their lanes. Compare these to the load's posted rate. Think twice if the rate seems too good to be true; watch out for broker's scams. On the flip side, knowing the average spot rate can keep you from accepting a rate that is too low for the load. If the load generally goes for $3 a mile, then why should you haul it for $2.25?

How many loads are available?

Load boards can help you plan your loads and backhauls. Check out the load availability at your drop-off location. How easy is it to get out of the area and/or back to your home location?

Learn about your Competition

Load boards also allow you to see how many posted trucks are in your lane. The search process is the same as above, but instead of searching for loads, you are searching for trucks.

How many trucks are in the area?

Knowing the number of available loads in a given area is only half the battle. You also need to know the number of available trucks. If an area has 300 available loads but only 50 available trucks, then you know there are roughly six loads per truck. You have some room to negotiate a better rate for your business. However, if 300 available trucks are trying to bid on 50 available loads, it is safe to say the freight rates are going to be lower.

Preparing to Negotiate Freight Rates

Negotiating freight is about supply and demand. If there are more available loads than trucks, you have a better shot at negotiating a higher freight rate. Use the load boards to help you keep track of market trends and make smart business decisions.

Know Your Financials

Your first step is to know whether or not a load is profitable for your company, which requires an understanding of your fleet's operating costs, available cash, and revenue. Many trucking companies lose money on loads because they do not pay enough attention to their financials. To avoid that trap, you need to calculate what range of load rates will make money for your company. What represents a good rate may change depending on the time of year, how much cash you have on hand, and what lanes you are running.

Develop Criteria

You need to write out a list of the most important qualities you need in a broker or a shipper. Your list may look something like this:

•Pays on time

•Good communicator

•Is direct and decisive

•Provides loads regularly

•Has a good reputation

•Is financially secure

Not every shipper or broker you work with will meet all of these requirements. However, having a list of criteria sets a standard for your company. Your list can help you focus on long-term business partners who can provide steady income.

Pick Your Lanes

When selecting loads, make sure they are in trucking lanes that work for your business. Keep in mind the expense of hauling through the Rockies and other rugged parts of the country. Choose shipments that allow you to make money on the way back home.

Check Credit Scores

Knowing the credit ratings and days-to-pay information on a broker or shipper improves your chances of making the right business decisions and getting paid on time.

Take a Strategic Approach to Load Boards

Do some research and look for load boards that offer good rates in the lanes you want to serve. Signing up on a handful of reliable boards increases your chances of getting the best loads. You will also want to post a profile about your company on each load board so that shippers have a way of finding authorities or fleet owners looking for brokers.

Finding loads to haul is always a big question. For contractors that are on their own and looking for freight to haul, a freight broker can help. Freight brokers connect shippers to truckers, and this is a nice option if you're just starting your own business. Freight brokers help to find loads for truckers and fleet owners. Brokers make it easy for independent professional truck drivers who are looking for quality loads because they always have a relationship with the shippers. Using freight brokers is an easy way to get loads for trucks, but their fees can be expensive.

Dispatch Services for Trucking Authorities and Fleet Owners.

Make use of dispatcher directly or contract with a dispatching service to connect you with brokers and shippers. Dispatchers can help provide administrative services like accounting, billing, and collections. While In other cases, they can provide back-office services that can help to ensure shippers pay invoices on time.

Load Boards.

Load boards are another means of connecting shippers to truckers. These boards can make it very easy to find loads by having multiple options to choose from, with the shipment details spelled out. It's best to find good load boards that meet your needs, so you're not wasting time. Most load board will allow free trials and have mobile apps so you can search for loads to haul and also send you notifications, so you never miss a high-paying load.

Networking.

Networking with fellow truckers is one of the easiest means of getting loads. Start by getting involved with industry associations and attending events that shippers and truckers are attending. The internet is also a great place to find out what is going on in the trucking industry. You want to find an industry that has the type of freight you're interested in. Joining an association may be the best idea for networking, or prospecting is your end goal. There are also opportunities for you to get referrals from people who work in your industry. Get to know people, and you'll be surprised at how this small industry is, and that can pay off in the future. Most of these associations can also provide you with tips on how to save money for your trucking business. Some of them even provide membership opportunities that help build a prospect list.

Broker Your Freight

The most complex way to find loads for your authority, but this require a substantial lead time. You will need to learn to be a broker, whether with an established broker or by taking some professional classes. It pays to broker freight, but it might not be a risk you're comfortable with.

Work Directly With Shippers

The most successful motor carriers of today developed most relationships with shippers and only make use of brokers or load boards for their backhauls. If You want to typically get paid more for loads without a middleman or like a broker., You can keep your profit margins up by working directly with shippers as often as you can.

What Clientele Do You Want

Before you start going after loads, you'll have to define the customer you want to work with. Knowing your target client will give you a clear perspective on what you want and how you can find them. There is never a perfect client, but you want to be able to find clients who are perfect for you.

Finding Your Loads

With the internet, you can find instant information by using load board websites. After a few clicks, they have the contact information to finalize the deal. The only disadvantage of a load board is that truck drivers will have to pay a monthly subscription fee for the service, and prices may vary depending on the level of service available through the site.

•Freight Brokers may allow drivers to reach the larger shipping public and get more consistent volumes customized to their equipment or location.

•Industry Associations – Another way to find clients is through industry associations with local branches in your area. You don't have to join these organizations; all you need to do is just get the list of their local members. Once you have the ideas, you can now call the clients and speak to the person in charge of shipping. Try to set up a meeting, determine how they select their carriers, and get on their list. Giving you an upper hand because while competitors are on load boards. You are doing the hard work and securing necessary clients directly to give you the highest paying freight loads.

Starting your own truck company is a good idea and helps build the economy. Once you find your freight, you're ready to grow. Though running your own company can be tasking, but when you find the right clients, everything will run smoothly.

It is best to try different ways to see what works best for you. Finding the best load board for your trucking company and dealing with freight brokers can help you become familiar with the opportunities in your area. Whatever option you choose, stick with it, and watch your trucking business grow.

Chapter 4: Negotiating Rates

As a carrier or a truck operator, rate negotiations can be annoying. It eats away at your time, energy levels, and mental state. But negotiating good rates is essential to a successful business. To be able to negotiate freight rates effectively, shippers need to know when and where to apply leverage. Here are some tips for you when negotiating with brokers to make sure you're getting the best rates possible.

Prepare to Negotiate

Before you start negotiating, You need to know what you need and what's available. Review market trends, Study the effects of currency rates, politics, and economics on the industry, Identify your volume needs and budget.

Compare Prices

Before you meet with your carrier, first find out what your competition is charging. Some price factors to compare may include:

• insurance

- Lead times
- Accessorial charges
- Transit requirements
- Weights and dimensions
- Origin and destination zip codes
- Spot rates, contract rates, and special project rates

As you train yourself to know more about the carrier's competition, you're more likely to earn concessions during negotiations. The carrier might be willing to reduce the fees if they think you might move to their competitor.

Don't Pay for What You Don't Use.

It is good to know the level of service, price, and security you want. Talk with your carrier about the kind of services they provide and pick what's relevant for you.

Let your carrier know what's important to you and point out what's not necessary.

Build Relationships

Your carrier is a necessary component of your supply chain. When negotiating freight rates, use your people skills to build positive long-term relationships. It is important to remember that the supply and demand between shippers and carriers are not constant.

Leverage Group Buying

By joining a buying group, you can leverage the collective buying power and get discounts. An advantage of group buying is that skilled negotiators can lock in rates for six months or more. More contracts make it easier to budget and predict your shipping costs.

Negotiate a Master Carrier Agreement

A master carrier agreement is a private contract that concerns only to you. The carrier doesn't offer the same terms to their other shippers. So, when you negotiate a master carrier agreement, your carrier won't be able to change tariffs or other terms without your approval.

Know Your Operating Cost

Before you start negotiating rates, you need to know how much it's going to cost to operate your business. Having the amount in mind will help so as not to accept rates that are below your operating costs, which may hurt your operation and even put your business at risk.

Pay Attention To Spot Rates.

Spot rates are a one-time rate for transporting any load. Spot rates can differ depending on the time of year, fuel prices, supply and demand, and more. Good load boards will have average spot rates for a particular load.

Know The Loads-To-Trucks Ratio.

Always know the number of trucks posted for the lane. If there's a large number of loads and a small number of trucks available, You have the room to ask for a better rate because trucks are in high demand. If you have more trucks than loads, then the rates will likely be lower with less room to negotiate. A good load board will give you the ability to see the information when you're negotiating rates.

Figure Out Your Cost Per Mile.

If you are not sure how much it costs to run your truck company and you have no idea what to charge to keep it on the road. If you're accepting rates that are less than your operating costs, then you'll run yourself out of business. You'll have to calculate your cost per mile, so you make good decisions while on the road.

Watch Load Times.

Time is a significant factor concerning load rates. The longer the load stays on a load board, the more anxious the broker will be. You can then use this opportunity to negotiate rates to your advantage. Also, you'll need to pay utmost attention to the pick-up time because the less time there is until the load needs to move, the more likely the broker needs a carrier stat.

Provide Good Customer Service.

Remember, both you and the broker are trying to get the best rate. You can't go wrong with good communication.

Ask Questions.

There's a lot more to know about the load than just the rate and the lane. Be sure to you ask:

• If you will be helping to load and unload.

• How long you'll be at the shipper.

• If the pay is by the pound, by unit or by foot, etc.

• If you're going to need anything specific like straps, etc.

These are a few of the questions; you might need to ask to make sure you're prepared.

Questions should be relevant and move toward your end goal.

Find Out If There Are Any Additional Fees.

Some lanes are more expensive to run. Ask questions about fees you know are likely to be an issue:

• Do you have to pay dock or lumper fees?

• Are there any tolls along the route?

• Is the fuel surcharge covered in the rate?

• Does the load require any special permits?

Make sure you ask anything that might be necessary regarding the shipper, receiver or late fees, etc.

Chapter 5: Paperwork And Documentation

Trucking companies are regulated by the Department of Transportation (DOT). To start up a trucking company, you must comply with state and federal business guidelines and follow the state rules for interstate and intrastate transport. While some documents stay at the office, other documents stay with each truck.

State Business Registration

Before you get to apply for the DOT license and any permits, you'll need to register as a business. This is done by visiting your local Secretary Of State's office or website. Once you have a business name and structures are properly registered, then your business entity is established.

Internal Revenue Service Tax Identification

Just like people have the Social Security numbers, businesses also have tax identification numbers. This is obtained through the IRS website, and this number can usually be obtained for free and immediately. It is needed when you open business bank accounts and apply for permits and licensing.

Class A Driver's License

The driver of the truck must maintain a valid Class A driver's license. Drivers must have a clean driving record and pass a drug test. The Class A driver's license is also known as the Commercial Driver's License, and it is obtained after taking a DMV-approved trucking class that covers the specific rules and regulations.

US DOT Number

This U.S. DOT number registers the business with the Department of Transportation. You be given this number and issued a provisional permit until you complete an 18-month New Entrant Safety Assurance Program. After completing the program, your number and permit become permanent. Originals should remain at the office, and copies should be placed on each truck as well.

Commercial Liability Insurance

An insurance policy is needed for the U.S. DOT approval. An individual must have a sum of $75,000 surety bond and general liability policy that protects you from liability and cargo loss at a minimum of $750,000. Insurance papers should be kept in the truck with the declarations pages maintained at the office.

Heavy Highway Use Tax Return, Form 2290

For trucks that are over 55,000 pounds, the IRS requires a special tax return for infrastructure budgets. You get credits if you drive fewer than 5,000 miles annually, but most big rigs are required to complete this form and pay the use tax.

State Transportation Permits

Each state has its cargo and transportation permit requirements. Check for your local DMV to see which permits are required for transport in your area. Be sure to keep any permits in the truck in case you are stopped and asked to produce them.

Chapter 6: Ongoing Fmcsa And Dot Compliance

Federal Motor Carrier Safety Administration (FMCSA)also known as Compliance, Safety, Accountability (CSA) is an initiative that helps to improve large truck and bus safety and also reduce crashes, injuries, and fatalities that are related to commercial vehicles. It presents a new law and compliance model that gives room for FMCSA and its State Partners to contact a large number of carriers at an early stage to address safety problems before crashes occur.

Rules For Safety

Truck drivers should know that the Department of Transportation issues DOT numbers that appear on various paperwork, indicating registration with the agency. DOT regulations govern every aspect of the industry.

Driver Training And Qualification

To agree with DOT regulations, Truck drivers must satisfy several conditions. Driver training includes both instruction and practice that is sufficient enough to earn a commercial driver's license. There's also a background check to make sure there are no violations of rules or convictions that would stop drivers from receiving their certification. In most cases, the licensing includes a physical exam and a medical test to verify that there are no disabilities that could contribute to unsafe vehicle operation.

Commercial driver licenses cover several categories. These can be related to the type or size (weight) of the vehicle, type of cargo, the number of passengers, and more.

Examples of these categories include :

•Vehicle size: The licenses Class A B C specifies the type of vehicle size or weight of the load carried, and other large vehicles single or in combination.

•Passengers: Class B licenses also allow operations of specialized passenger vehicles such as school buses or city buses, while Class C licenses are acceptable for commercial drivers with smaller passenger vehicles.

•Hazmat: Vehicles transporting hazardous materials, which involves certain restrictions.

Drug And Alcohol Testing

This is a standard part of the drivers' experience. DOT rules require that drivers should be aware of the rules and regulations and that they are subject to random testing. The Standards for drug and alcohol testing also apply to supervisors, who receive training in how to recognize signs of substance abuse.

Record Keeping

The ELD rule is part of the changes concerning the driver's hours of service, there rules and regulations that are continually updated and revised.

Other forms of documentation that fall under DOT regulatory control include:

•Bills of lading and manifests
•Dispatch and trip records
•Expense receipts (including toll charges)
•Fleet management communications
•Payroll records and settlement sheets

Load (Cargo) Securing

Commercial vehicles that carry cargos take many forms, from tractor-trailer to flatbeds. The Department of Transportation has established guidelines and rules that dictate how the load is to be distributed and the proper methods for securing it are in place to prevent dangerous load shifting, vehicle overturning, or accidental dumping or spillage.

Licenses And Permits

This category includes several rules and regulations that also specify taxes (on fuel and vehicle use), on the federal and state level. It includes specifics such as weight restrictions and types of vehicle licenses. Licenses and permits include:

•IRP – International Registration Plan, for payment of license fees

•IFTA – International Fuel Tax Agreement, for payment of fuel taxes

•Straight plates – for in-state driving

•Single-trip permit applications

Transporting Hazardous Materials

Rules govern the transport of hazardous materials: substances they're comprised of, and the types of vehicles allowed to carry it, The placards to be displayed on the vehicle when the material is being carried. DOT can also stop vehicles that are transporting these substances from using some roads or from entering some designated areas.

Vehicle Inspection

Commercial vehicles get regular inspections from both the authorities and the drivers themselves. DOT established a program of pre- and post-movement inspections. It requires that a vehicle inspection form be submitted when an equipment or safety issue is discovered. Stating the nature of the problem; and if the repairs have been made.

Ensuring Dot Compliance

The Federal Motor Carrier Safety Administration (FMCSA) as provided a web page for carriers and drivers that enable them to find out if they need DOT registration and allows them to apply for it online

How to be DOT compliant?

DOT compliance means successfully meeting up with the requirements of the U.S. Department of Transportation, the federal agency that enforces rules (DOT regulations) governing the operation of commercial motor vehicles. Failure to be DOT compliant results in a violation of these rules. Violators are subjected to sanctions that might include fines, suspension of a company's permission to operate, or jail time.

Who Must Comply

The DOT rules and regulations apply to vehicles that are required to register with the DOT and receive a USDOT number.

These are the commercial vehicles with specifically the DOT guidelines that concern motor vehicles operating under one or more of these criteria:

- Transportation of hazardous materials.
- A vehicle weight rating of 4,536 kg (10,001 pounds) or more
- Transportation of more than eight passengers (including the
    driver) for compensation
- Transportation of more than 15 passengers, including the driver

These qualifications are for vehicles that are used for interstate commerce. Some states require intrastate commercial vehicle owners to obtain a USDOT number.

Compliance Procedure: Know The Rules

To be sure that commercial drivers and carriers are in compliance with the DOT rules, where to start is with the regulations within themselves.

Sample Checklists

After getting familiar with the regulations, commercial drivers can now stay on track and avoid lapses by regularly reviewing their operations. The following checklists provide useful guidelines to ensure adherence to DOT standards for drivers and fleet managers.

Fleet Compliance

○ Maintain a copy of the current FMCSA rules in the office.

○ Complete pre-trip and post-trip inspections of vehicles, with

documentation.

○ Develop a vehicle maintenance program and adhere to it with documentation.

- Ensure that each vehicle is marked with your companies DOT related numbers.

- Maintain a record of any road incidents for each vehicle.

DRIVER COMPLIANCE
- Provide each driver with a copy of FMCSA rules, and obtain
  a signed receipt for the document and agreement to follow the regulations described in it.
- Maintain qualification records and safety history for each driver.
- Maintain a record of HOS (hours of service) for each driver.
- Maintain records of pre-employment drug testing for each driver. This should also include reports of drug and alcohol abuse in previous employment, if any.
- Conduct random drug and alcohol testing of drivers on a regular basis, as described in DOT regulations.
- Require supervisors to receive drug and alcohol training as required by DOT regulations.

The checklist covers the necessary aspects of DOT compliance, but to make sure that all requirements are met, a commercial fleet owner needs to become thoroughly acquainted with DOT regulations and make the appropriate adjustments to the organization's policy and operations. These regular reviews can help minimize the risk of noncompliance.

Chapter 7: Consortiums And Drug Testing

Drug testing programs are available for both DOT Employers and trucking authorities. The U.S. Drug Test Centers are experts at establishing and administering DOT-compliant testing programs for any business in the transportation industry. If your company is regulated by the DOT, you're required to have a DOT-compliant drug and alcohol test in place.

Drug testing programs are necessary for employers who are regulated by the United States Department of Transportation (DOT). As a trucking authority, you are required to go through a consortium drug testing program. Smaller DOT-regulated employers should also go through a consortium drug testing program for easy compliance.

The Federal Motor Carrier Safety Administration (FMCSA), along with the Department of Transportation (DOT), requires that persons subject to the commercial driver's license (CDL) requirements and their employers follow alcohol and drug testing rules. These rules include procedures for testing, frequency of tests, and substances tested for.

Who's Impacted?

•Anyone employing CDL drivers to operate commercial motor vehicles (CMVs) on public roads

•CDL drivers who operate CMVs on public roads

•Interstate motor carriers

•Intrastate motor carriers

•Federal, state, and local governments

•Civic organizations (disabled veteran transport, boy/girl scouts, etc.)

•Faith-based organizations

Resources for Drivers

While it is the responsibility of your employer to provide you with information on drug and alcohol testing programs, it is still ultimately your responsibility to obey all rules and regulations in order to keep our roadways safe. Drivers of CMVs can learn about drug and alcohol rules, types of tests required, and their rights, responsibilities, and requirements here.

Resources for Employers

As an employer, you have a responsibility to implement and conduct drug and alcohol testing programs. Learn about drug and alcohol rules and how they affect your business here.

*An employer who employs himself/herself as a driver must comply with requirements of 49 CFR Part 382 that apply to both employers and drivers.

Resources for Service Agents

Service agents that administer drug and alcohol tests can find general information and other resources here.

Guidance on Drug and Alcohol Supervisor Training

All persons designated to supervise drivers of commercial motor vehicles that require a commercial driver's license can find information and resources here on who is required to take Drug and Alcohol Supervisor Training.

DOT Audits and Compliance

The U.S. Drug Test Centers can help truck operators that are regulated by any of the DOT agencies with compliant drug and alcohol testing programs. It's necessary that you work with an experienced C/TPA for your drug testing needs. Ask your vendors if they can help you possibly help you in the event of an audit or program review. You must have the following:

- Alcohol and drug testing policies, and instructions for implementing your program

- Employee and supervisor training records
- Records of drug testing custody and control forms for all DOT required tests

- MRO records
- Alcohol testing forms for all DOT tests
- Employee return-to-duty records

Noncompliance can result in fines of up to $10,000 per event and the possibility of an out-of-service order, putting your authority out of business. Violations happen when the company:

- Doesn't have drug and alcohol testing policy

- Doesn't have a stand-alone or a testing consortium program
- Is making use of a driver who has not completed a drug test
- Is making use of a driver who as refused a required alcohol
    or drug test
- Is making use of a driver who has previously tested positive
    and has not completed a return-to-duty process as
    required by a Substance Abuse Professional (SAP)

Consortium Testing Program
- This is a drug testing pool that involves multiple companies
- All employees from different companies are enrolled in the consortium and are eligible for selection for a drug or alcohol test
- Once the necessary testing percentages are met, all companies in the consortium are in compliance
- Perfect for trucking authorities
- This is a drug testing pool with employees from just one company

- Companies with more than 12 employees are eligible to have

  a stand-alone random testing program

- Testing programs are also available for bus companies,
  private fleets and for-hire carriers.

DOT Required Testing

Trucking authority

For trucking authorities, two important steps must be carried out to comply with the DOT FMCSA regulations for drug and alcohol testing:

1   A pre-employment drug test with a negative result must be completed before operating a DOT covered commercial motor vehicle (CMV)

121

2   The owner must enroll in a random testing consortium. Small trucking authorities are not permitted to manage random testing themselves

Why is Consortium Enrollment Important?

The consortium is important to save time and money, to avoid fines and out-of-service violations. Fines can be up to $10,000 per occurrence.

For new truck-operators, within 12 months after beginning operations, you will get a DOT FMCSA safety audit, which is often called a new entrant examination. Audits and compliance reviews include verification of your DOT FMCSA drug and alcohol testing program. A new trucking authority will automatically fail the safety audit for violations related to:

- Trucking authority not enrolled in a consortium program for drug and alcohol testing
- Owners that have No alcohol and/or drug testing program
- Making use of a driver who refused a required alcohol or drug test
- Making use of a driver the company knows had a blood alcohol content of 0.05 or greater
- Making use of a driver who failed to complete necessary

follow-up procedures after testing positive for drugs.

For truck operators, two important steps need to be taken to comply with the DOT FMCSA regulations for drug and alcohol testing:

1   A pre-employment drug test with a negative result must be completed before operating a DOT covered commercial motor vehicle (CMV)

2   You must enroll in a random testing consortium. Trucking authorities are not permitted to manage random testing themselves.

The U.S. Drug Test Centers can make easy the process of drug and alcohol testing and help your company with a program that keeps you in compliance and out of trouble with the DOT so that you avoid fines and penalties.

What is Necessary for DOT Drug and Alcohol Testing Compliance?

The U.S. Drug Test Centers can help Authorities with all of the required components of a compliant DOT drug and alcohol testing program.

•Designated Employer Representative (DER)

•Written policy

•Regulations on file

•Pre-employment testing

•Random, post-accident, reasonable suspicion, return-to-duty, and follow-up testing

•Employee education

•Supervisor training

•Previous employer checks

•Removal of employees from safety-sensitive positions when positive or refusal to test

•Substance Abuse Professional

What About the Other DOT Agencies?

The U.S. Drug Test Centers can provide DOT-compliant drug and alcohol testing programs for all of the various DOT agencies, which include:

•   Federal Aviation Admin (FAA)

•   Federal Railroad Admin (FRA)

•   Federal Transit Admin (FTA)

124

- Pipeline & Hazardous Materials Safety Administration (PHMSA)
- United States Coast Guard (USCG)
- Federal Motor Carrier Safety Admin (FMCSA)

Both the DOT agency and the USCG have rules and regulations that require certain employers to implement a random testing program. Compliance experts at the U.S. Drug Test Centers can help you go around through the requirements for your DOT required random drug testing program

Chapter 8: Your first year and seasoning your authority

The ability to travel around on a regular basis and make money while doing something you love is an opportunity and a dream. Very few employment positions that have this opportunity are truck drivers. Drivers deliver items from all around the world throughout the U.S. and sometimes even Other states. Truck drivers are an essential part of our everyday life for almost every industry. Beginner truck drivers have the opportunity to see the country and also have the opportunity to develop their driving skills.

There are many advantages of having your own authority and being your own boss, setting your own schedule, choosing loads and lanes that suit you, leaving company politics. But where there is much freedom, there is much responsibility. Following these tips from others' who have been there and have had experience will improve your chances of being a success in your first year on your own.

Though starting a trucking authority gives more opportunity to make more money. In your first year, what to expect is to lay out a lot of cash for your working capital, out-of-pocket expenses, insurance, meals, repairs, and other expenses. You will have to do a lot of research to get an accurate handle on both expected income and expenses.

Your ways of spending and managing money will determine your success as a trucking authority. It is good to set ambitious goals, but you can't keep spending and anticipating future growth. Your budget should be based on yearlong averages.

Get or lease trucks you're sure you can afford and also set aside money for insurance, repairs, and maintenance and even for a brand new truck.

Whether you're making use of a brand new or used truck, do your homework and align the engine with the load you expect to carry. Always consider the truck's fuel economy and its age for the money. Get inputs from other experienced trucking authorities with similar trucks and engines. It also focuses on longevity and reliability, as well as maintenance requirements and overall performance.

In the first year as a new trucking authority, you'll experience the common mistake of becoming an independent trucker with bad credit or excessive personal debts, which you would have to avoid. Also, you'll have to Minimize your credit card debt. Maintaining good credit can support your ability to keep rolling; and access the necessary capital for equipment, fuel cards, and investment in your business.

Set aside money for downtime and emergencies.
You'll have to Plan for rainy days by setting aside a little bit each week, "just in case." Work dries up, or You fall sick.

Make Consultations with experts on accounting and legal issues to set up the appropriate business structure for your trucking authority. Keep proper records and plan for taxes and address various legal issues. Seek out reputable experts who can give proper advice.

If you're going to be on the road for a long time, you have to have good health. If you are down because you have health issues, you are not going to make enough making money. If you've got health issues, plan for getting medicals If you've got health issues. Make sure you have a good health insurance policy and be prepared to pay for travel coverage.

Whether you are new to the industry or maybe you have been leased on to a company for years, you have to stay one step ahead of your competition. Connect with industry leaders and learn from them. These connections can help grow your business. You'll also need to go for professional training.

Owning a truck authority is a business, and your truck is your tool. You have to always be ready. In case something happens to your truck, or you need more money for fuel. These are your new responsibilities. Also, when evaluating loads, always strike the right balance between home time and having enough cash coming in. Know what you're getting into before you sign. Focus on building long-term relationships with good customers

As a business owner, you'll want your venture to grow and compete with the leaders of the industry. You're in luck, as there are five essential tips on how to grow your trucking company.

1. Think Outside the Box

Holding on to just one customer is hardly going to be the most successful route to growth. To grow your business, you are going to have to build a network of customers rather than basing the stability of your business on one manufacturer or one broker. Building a list of your own clients and working with different types of clients can help your trucking company have a sense of reliability, which will go far in acquiring more clients in the long run, and therefore grow your business.

A good way to go about this is to visit the local manufacturers in your area, present your business as the solution to all their transportation needs, and build relationships with them. Not all manufacturers considered need to become clients, only the ones that seem the most profitable and beneficial for business have to stay on the client list. It may seem like a tedious task at first with mediocre loads, but building relationships with the right clients will give you a basis to command better rates and a good reputation that'll give you better standing when attempting to approach more clients in the future.

2. Determine Your Costs

Before you can save money, you need to know how much you're required to spend.

First, what are your regular costs? Next, calculate your variable costs, such as fuel and subtract your total cost from your rates, and you'll get your profits. Once you have this, you can set goals for how to increase it going forward.

3. Make Sure The Paperwork Is In Order

The office is not a revenue-producing part of a small trucking business, and therefore it can often be the most neglected. Especially for small fleet owners, it's easy to see the paperwork as an unimportant part of the business that can easily be done when it is desperately needed. However, a well-run office equals a well-run trucking business. Constantly monitoring things like routing and fuel, as well as dispatch and planning tools, can really increase the profitability of a business without having to increase your load.

To make handling paperwork even easier, there are companies like Authority Express LLC who can allow you to stay on top of paperwork without having to add back-office staff to the payroll. This means you can prevent fines and delays by avoiding mistakes and spend the valuable time you would've spent filing paperwork to secure your next load and grow your trucking business.

4. Organize a load board

Another way to grow your business is to start using load boards. As a small fleet owner, you'll be spending time building relationships with shippers, and you most likely won't have constant work scheduled, so load boards are a safe bet to tide you over when loads are sparse. Using multiple load boards at once, such as DAT, Sure Way, and Truck Stop, can ensure you get the best rates for your needs and capacity. You can also pick up loads with the Federal government, such as the U.S. General Services Administration, Federal Business Opportunities, and the U.S Postal Service. Remember to not make load boards something you rely on; your main priority is to build your own relationships with shippers to create the stability that working with different shippers too often from load boards cannot. However, this does take time, so, until then, organize a load board until you have established enough relationships where you won't have to rely on load boards.

5. Buy Fuel Correctly

Fuel can often be the biggest expense of a trucking business, with over 53.9 billion gallons being used annually, so you need to make sure you are buying fuel in the most cost-efficient way possible. New and experienced truckers alike have the tendency to buy fuel as if they are a normal driver, in that they think that they will pay taxes based on the state where the fuel was purchased. However, truck drivers pay taxes on their fuel differently as they deal with the International Tax Fund and get taxed on the amount of fuel used on the journey (in each particular state-driven through), regardless of which state the fuel was originally bought from. This is why it is better not to buy fuel based on the lowest pump price but rather based on the lowest base price.

Growing any business can be tough, but by following these tips, you should be able to take your trucking business to the next level, ensuring more stability and profitability, making the most out of your opportunity to create a successful company of your own.

Support The Right Market Niche

The most important step to be a successful trucking authority is to support the right market niche. This step affects small fleet owners as well. The market you choose determines the equipment you buy, the rates you charge, and the freight lanes you can service.

As a rule, trucking authorities should focus on markets that the large carriers avoid. In other words, consider hauling specialized loads.

Making decent revenues with a dry van is very difficult as a trucking authority. There is too much competition from large carriers and other trucking authorities trying to pull the "easier" loads.

There are many markets that you can focus on. However, hauling fresh produce and meat in reefers has many advantages, including less competition, year-round work, and it's resistant to recessions. The last one is very important.

2. Charge the right rate (per mile)

As a trucking authority, you need to determine what rate to charge your clients to haul a load. Your rates need to be high enough to give you a nice profit and pay all your operation costs. You need to know your rates before you start calling shippers and making sales. Remember, when you call shippers, you want to be competitive with what brokers charge them.

There is a simple way to do this:

1.Select your freight lane

2.Go to a load board

3.Find 10 loads going in one direction

4.Call the brokers and find out how much they pay

5.Get the average

6.Add 10% to 15% to get the price brokers charge shippers

7.Repeat the process for the opposite direction

Now you know how much the lane pays for a round trip – taking and bringing loads back. We outline this process in detail (and provide a great tool) in this article: "Determine your rates (per mile)."

Work Directly With Shippers

Load boards and brokers have their place in your business. They can be very useful when you have an empty truck. However, they are also very expensive. Brokers keep about

134

10% to 20% of the load price. That's fair, as they must make a living, and they provide the shipper (and you) with a service. Minimize your use of brokers and load boards. Instead, develop a client list of direct shippers. Done right, you can develop a list of reliable shippers that will keep you busy. Charge them a price that is competitive to what brokers charge – but keep everything for yourself instead. We have written the following resources to help you grow your shipper list:

Run an efficient back office

Having an efficient back office is key if you want to stay profitable and grow. The importance of the back office becomes more important as you start adding leased drivers to your operation. You have a couple of options.

One option is to do it yourself. You can run your business out of the cab of your truck. All you need is a laptop, an Internet connection, and a printer. You also need accounting software to run your business. There are several options on the market. One well-known solution is Truckbytes, which offers a free entry-level package.

Alternatively, you can outsource your back office to a dispatcher. However, they can be expensive. If you choose this route, interview them thoroughly. The wrong dispatcher can kill your business.

7. Avoid cash flow problems

Trucking is a cash flow-intensive business. You are always buying fuel, making insurance payments, making truck payments, and so on. Unless you get quick-pays, shippers and brokers can pay invoices in 15 to 30 days. Sometimes they take 45 days. This delay can create a cash flow problem for you, especially in the early days of the business.

One way around this problem is to use freight bill factoring. Factoring solves your cash flow problem by advancing up to 95% of the invoice, often the day you submit it. The remaining 5%, less a small fee, is rebated once your shipper pays. Many factoring companies provide fuel advances, cards, and other services as well. By the way, we are a factoring company. If you need factoring, fill out this form, and a credit manager will contact you shortly.

Maurice Sanders is a serial entrepreneur. He is an eternal optimist and has a knack for adventure. Having seen his fair share of ups and downs in life, he continues to develop businesses and jumpstart new ventures. He also possesses a interest in teaching entrepreneurial skills at the Chicago Urban League. Maurice holds a bachelor's degree in Computer Science and Marketing from Northern Illinois University.

A couple of his favorite quotes include:

"Success is the progressive step towards a worthy goal"

"You will be the same person in five years as you are today except for the people you meet and the books you read"

When he is not working, he is sculpting or coaching new entrepreneurs into launching successful business ventures. He also enjoys travelling and thinking about his next journey in life.

Are you're looking for help in reaching your life or business goals?

Visit mauricethefirst.com or contact Maurice directly at maurice@mauricethefirst.com to invest in one on coaching, courses or other products to help you reach the next level. Such as our bookkeeping software to help you keep track of revenue and expenses in a simple, efficient and organized manner.

Check out Maurice's other books:

The Bullseye Approach: Starting A Company Now

The Teens Business Bible: Helping Kids Start Their Own Business

Reference

https://www.teletracnavman.com/resources/resource-library/faqs/how-to-be-dot-compliant

https://smallbusiness.chron.com/documents-needed-open-truck-company-37217.html

https://ezfreightfactoring.com/blog/pros-cons-trucking-trucking authority

https://www.turnkeyauthority.com/10-steps-trucking-authority/
https://www.motorcarrierhq.com/2015/06/24/finding-your-freight/

https://ecapital.com/6-ways-to-find-more-loads-for-your-trucking-business/

https://www.dat.com/trucking   authoritys/get-authority/carrier-startup-guide

https://www.tafs.com/negotiating-freight-rates/

https://www.usdrugtestcenters.com/dot-consortium-random-drug-testing.html

https://www.invoicefactoring.com/factoring-blog/trucking/how-to-make-it-through-your-first-year-as-an-trucking authority

https://owneroperatorland.com/blog/pros-and-cons-of-trucking authority-trucking/

https://www.rtsinc.com/articles/how-get-loads-pay-well

https://www.comcapfactoring.com/blog/how-to-make-a-successful-trucking-company-one-important-tip